Quod scriptura, non iubet vetat

The Latin translates, "What is not commanded in scripture, is forbidden:'

On the Cover: Baptists rejoice to hold in common with other evangelicals the main principles of the orthodox Christian faith. However, there are points of difference and these differences are significant. In fact, because these differences arise out of God's revealed will, they are of vital importance. Hence, the barriers of separation between Baptists and others can hardly be considered a trifling matter. To suppose that Baptists are kept apart solely by their views on Baptism or the Lord's Supper is a regrettable misunderstanding. Baptists hold views which distinguish them from Catholics, Congregationalists, Episcopalians, Lutherans, Methodists, Pentecostals, and Presbyterians, and the differences are so great as not only to justify, but to demand, the separate denominational existence of Baptists. Some people think Baptists ought not teach and emphasize their differences but as E.J. Forrester stated in 1893, "Any denomination that has views which justify its separate existence, is bound to promulgate those views. If those views are of sufficient importance to justify a separate existence, they are important enough to create a duty for their promulgation ... the very same reasons which justify the separate existence of any denomination make it the duty of that denomination to teach the distinctive doctrines upon which its separate existence rests." If Baptists have a right to a separate denominational life, it is their duty to propagate their distinctive principles, without which their separate life cannot be justified or maintained.

Many among today's professing Baptists have an agenda to revise the Baptist distinctives and redefine what it means to be a Baptist. Others don't understand why it even matters. The books being reproduced in the *Baptist Distinctives Series* are republished in order that Baptists from the past may state, explain and defend the primary Baptist distinctives as they understood them. It is hoped that this Series will provide a more thorough historical perspective on what it means to be distinctively Baptist.

The Lord Jesus Christ asked, *"And why call ye me, Lord, Lord, and do not the things which I say?"* (Luke 6:46). The immediate context surrounding this question explains what it means to be a true disciple of Christ. Addressing the same issue, Christ's question is meant to show that a confession of discipleship to the Lord Jesus Christ is inconsistent and untrue if it is not accompanied with a corresponding submission to His authoritative commands. Christ's question teaches us that a true recognition of His authority as Lord inevitably includes a submission to the authority of His Word. Hence, with this question Christ has made it forever impossible to separate His authority as King from the authority of His Word. These two principles—the authority of Christ as King and the authority of His Word—are the two most fundamental Baptist distinctives. The first gives rise to the second and out of these two all the other Baptist distinctives emanate. As F.M. Iams wrote in 1894, "Loyalty to Christ as King, manifesting itself in a constant and unswerving obedience to His will as revealed in His written Word, is the real source of all the Baptist distinctives:' In the search for the *primary* Baptist distinctive many have settled on the Lordship of Christ as the most basic distinctive. Strangely, in doing this, some have attempted to separate Christ's Lordship from the authority of Scripture, as if you could embrace Christ's authority without submitting to what He commanded. However, while Christ's Lordship and Kingly authority can be isolated and considered essentially for discussion's sake, we see from Christ's own words in Luke 6:46 that His Lordship is really inseparable from His Word and, with regard to real Christian discipleship, there can be no practical submission to the one without a practical submission to the other.

In the symbol above the Kingly Crown and the Open Bible represent the inseparable truths of Christ's Kingly and Biblical authority. The Crown and Bible graphics are supplemented by three Bible verses (Ecclesiastes 8:4, Matthew 28:18-20, and Luke 6:46) that reiterate and reinforce the inextricable connection between the authority of Christ as King and the authority of His Word. The truths symbolized by these components are further emphasized by the Latin quotation - *quod scriptura, non iubet vetat*— *i.e.,* "What is not commanded in scripture, is forbidden:' This Latin quote has been considered historically as a summary statement of the regulative principle of Scripture. Together these various symbolic components converge to exhibit the two most foundational Baptist Distinctives out of which all the other Baptist Distinctives arise. Consequently, we have chosen this composite symbol as a logo to represent the primary truths set forth in the *Baptist Distinctives Series.*

THE BAPTISM

OF THE AGES

AND OF THE NATIONS.

WILLIAM CATHCART
1826-1908

THE BAPTISM

OF THE AGES

AND OF THE NATIONS.

BY

WILLIAM CATHCART, D.D.,

AUTHOR OF "THE FATAL SYSTEM," AND OF "THE BAPTISTS
AND THE AMERICAN REVOLUTION."

With a Biographical Sketch of the Author by John Franklin Jones

PHILADELPHIA:
AMERICAN BAPTIST PUBLICATION SOCIETY
1120 CHESTNUT STREET.
1878

he Baptist Standard Bearer, Inc.

NUMBER ONE IRON OAKS DRIVE • PARIS, ARKANSAS 72855

Thou hast given a *standard* to them that fear thee;
that it may be displayed because of the truth.
— *Psalm 60:4*

Reprinted 2006

by

THE BAPTIST STANDARD BEARER, INC.
No. 1 Iron Oaks Drive
Paris, Arkansas 72855
(479) 963-3831

THE WALDENSIAN EMBLEM
lux lucet in tenebris
"The Light Shineth in the Darkness"

ISBN# 1579784062

PREFACE.

THE primary object which claimed the attention of the writer of this little work when he began its preparation was to secure and record reliable information about the *mode of baptism* used by the great missionaries who planted Christianity among the pagan communities now constituting the chief nations of the earth. How did St. Remigius baptize Clovis and his three thousand soldiers? How did St. Patrick baptize the Irish? How did St. Augustine baptize King Ethelbert and ten thousand of his subjects? How did Paulinus baptize the thronging thousands of Englishmen whom he was the means of converting in Northumberland? How did Boniface baptize his hundred thousand Germans? How did St. Anschar baptize the Scandinavians? How were the whole people of Kieff baptized when their Russian master, Vladimir the Great, just rescued from heathenism, ordered them to become Christians? The work has expanded beyond the original plan, and it is chiefly a book of facts and baptismal testimonies.

Baptism of the Ages. Frontispiece.
Page 29.
BAPTISTERY OF BISHOP PAULINUS.

INTRODUCTION.

The name of the work, "THE BAPTISM OF THE AGES AND OF THE NATIONS," has been chosen because it describes its contents. Its pages afford ample evidence that for twelve centuries immersion was the baptism of *all* Christian countries, whether the climate was bitterly cold or intensely hot, and that it is the baptism of about a fourth part of all who bear the Christian name to-day. And the author has by no means exhausted this evidence by the large amount of it placed before his readers.

The important portions of this work were written by the Latin and Greek Fathers, by historians, schoolmen, monks, bishops, archbishops, cardinals, and popes of the Roman Catholic Church—men who are ranked among her most honored sons and holiest saints—and by eminent clergymen, travellers, and other authors of modern Protestant communities. In short, all that is valuable in the book was written by some of the leading men of all the Christian ages, and in a few cases by the inspired penmen themselves.

No *special* effort has been made to secure descriptions of baptism and of baptisms from Greek Christian writers, and some valuable testimony from these sources has been designedly passed by, because it is universally known by well-informed persons that immersion is now, and ever has been, the baptism of the Greek Church and of all other considerable Eastern Christian communities. Nevertheless, every part of Christendom is represented in these pages, either by creeds, by leading men teaching immersion, or by the immersion of candidates for baptism.

The quotations so frequently used in the following pages are all sustained by reliable authorities.

The meaning of "baptizo" is never discussed. Efforts in that field can add nothing to the results already obtained. The sole object of this work is to present narratives or descriptions of baptism by immersion in all countries—a field largely neglected by Baptists.

The work is divided into geographical, not chronological, sections. The baptismal records of each country are placed together, and for this reason the earliest baptisms are not found on the first pages.

In common with all regular Baptists, the writer firmly believes in salvation *by faith alone—by faith in the merits and imputed righteousness of the glorious*

INTRODUCTION. 7

Redeemer. But he denies the authority of any being *outside the eternal throne to alter in any particular*, or to set aside, any precept ever given by the sovereign Lamb. As the Roman Catholic wafer without the cup is a counterfeit, and not the Lord's Supper which it claims to be, so baptism without immersion is not the baptism the Saviour received in the river Jordan. It is a mere human contrivance, with less resemblance to Christ's baptism than the Romanist wafer bears to the Lord's Supper. This little work has been prepared to extend the practice of baptizing those only *whose sins have been already washed away by faith in the Saviour's blood*, and who in immersion solemnly and symbolically profess their burial and resurrection with Christ.

The writer is greatly indebted to the "Bucknell Library" of Crozer Theological Seminary for the use of its very valuable collection of the ecclesiastical writings of all ages—literary treasures of the highest worth. For facilities in the use of the library he is under lasting obligations to his friend the honored President of the Seminary, and to the other professors.

He has also received important assistance from the noble library of the American Baptist Historical Society.

His grateful acknowledgments are due to the

INTRODUCTION.

Rev. Dr. A. N. Arnold of Chicago, the Rev. Dr. H. Malcom, the Rev. A. J. Rowland, the Rev. Dr. G. W. Anderson, the Rev. J. S. Gubelmann, and Alfred T. Jones, Esq., editor of *The Jewish Record*, Philadelphia, and to several other friends in Europe and America, for valuable articles and information.

Praying that the heavenly Head of the militant Church, who honored immersion by observing it himself in the river Jordan, may bless this effort to the advancement of his gospel, we commit it to the examination of all who love the *truth as it is in Jesus*.

CONTENTS.

PAGE

TRINE IMMERSION...................................... 5

ENGLAND.

The English.—Their Pagan state in 596.—Bertha.—Augustine in Kent.—Baptism of the Ten Thousand.—Gregory's Letter to Eulogius.—Three witnesses: Fuller, Green, Tradition.—The Swale in Kent.—Gocelin and the Ten Thousand.—Importance of this Baptism.—Baptism of King Edwin and many others.—The Spring in York in which it Occurred.—Three Thousand Baptized in a Spring at Harbottle.—The Statue of Paulinus.—The Crucifix and Inscription.—Tradition.—Camden.—The Old Memory.—Paulinus Baptizes for Thirty-six Days in the River Glen and in the Swale.—He Baptizes a Multitude in the Trent.—The Mercians Baptized.—Caedwalla Immersed at Rome.—Bede and his Baptism.—The Council of Celichyth and Immersion.—Fridegod and Immersion.—Ethelred's Immersion.—Ancient Font.—Anlaf, a Royal Robber, is Immersed.—Lanfranc and Immersion.—Cardinal Pullus and Immersion.—The Christening of Prince Arthur and of the Princess Margaret.—Immersion in the time of "Bloody Mary."—Immersion in 1644.—Immersion in the Westminster Assembly of Divines.—Lightfoot's Journal.—Coleman.—Marshall.—Westminster Assembly's Commentary.—Dr. Chalmers.—Cave's Descrip-

10 CONTENTS.

PAGE

tion of Early Baptism.—The Manual of Sarum.—Bingham's Description of Early Baptism.—Milman and Immersion.—Maitland and Immersion.—Bradford Episcopal Church Baptistery.—Immersion compulsory in the State Church in England if demanded. 18

IRELAND.

St. Patrick Baptizes Hercus and many Thousand others.—He Baptizes the Amalgaidhs and Twelve Thousand Men in the well Tobur-en-Adare.—Many Converts Baptized at a Fountain.—Another Baptism of St. Patrick near Dublin.—Usher Mentions it.—Immersions Recorded by O'Farrell.—The Irish Immersed three times.—An Irish Bishop and Immersion.......................... 62

AMERICA.

John Wesley Immerses a Child in Georgia.—He seemingly Refuses to Sprinkle another.—A Baptism by Henry Ward Beecher in his Church.—Professor Lyman Coleman on Immersion as "*the first* Departure from the Teaching and Example of the Apostles".... 71

FRANCE.

Clovis and the Franks.—Clovis and the Battle of Zülpich.—Christ on the Side of Clovis.—Avitus on the Baptism of Clovis.—Gregory of Tours on the Battle-prayer of Clovis.—Clotilda.—Remigius.—The Baptism of Clovis and of Three Thousand Soldiers.—Gregory's Mode of Baptism.—Alcuin on the Baptism of Clovis.—Alcuin's Letter to the Canons of Lyons on Baptism.—Hincmar's Account of the Baptism of Clovis, his Army, his Sisters, and others.—His Baptistery.—Archbishop Magnus of Sens on Immersion.—Leidradus, Bishop of Lyons, on Immersion.—Theodulphus, Bishop of Orleans, on Im-

CONTENTS. 11

PAGE

mersion.—Hincmar of Rheims on Immersion.—Immersion of Hastein, a Danish Pirate.—Immersion of another Pirate.—St. Fulbert and Immersion.—Ivo, Bishop of Chartres, on Immersion.—Hugo of St. Victor on Immersion.—Abelard and Immersion.—Peter Lombard and Immersion.—Dupin and Immersion.... 79

SPAIN.

St. Isidore on Immersion.—The Fourth Council of Toledo on Immersion... 105

SWEDEN AND DENMARK.

St. Anschar.—His Character, his Baptisms.—Poppo's Baptizing Brook.. 109

GERMANY.

Boniface, the Missionary.—Othlon.—Pope Gregory II.—Pope Zacharias.—Boniface Baptizes many Thousands. —Samson the Irishman.—Pope Zacharias and Immersion. — The Oath of Boniface.—Willibrord Baptizes Three Men in a Fountain.—Alcuin's Standing.—Spain and One Immersion.—The Fathers favored Trine Immersion.—Alcuin doubts the Genuineness of the Letter of Gregory the Great to Leander.—Kohlrausch Sprinkles the Saxons in a River.—Alcuin's "Divine Offices." —Two Bishops describe Baptism to Charlemagne.—Rabanus Maurus and Trine Immersion.—Haymo and Immersion.—Wilafrid Strabo and Immersion.—Supposed Cases of Pouring.—Regino and Immersion.—St. Bruno and Immersion. — Otto Immerses Seven Thousand in Pomerania.—Rupert and Immersion.—Luther and Immersion... 112

SWITZERLAND.

Calvin and Immersion... 132

ITALY.

Clinic Baptism *for* Death.—First Baptism *for Death* was Pouring.—It was Defective for some Offices if the Person Recovered.—Cave, Eusebius, Pope Cornelius, Novatian, the Council of Neo-Cæsarea, Chrysostom.—Called "Clinics" in mockery, instead of Christians.—Cyprian defends Clinics.—Its Decline after Infant Baptism sprang up.—Immersion of a Paralyzed Jew in A. D. 408 in Constantinople.—Martyrdom the Second Baptism *for Death.*—Cyprian.—Immersion only for those likely to Live.—Justin Martyr on Immersion.—Ambrose on Immersion.—Pope Leo the Great and Immersion.—St. Maximus of Turin and Immersion.—Arator on Immersion.—Gregory the Great.—Arian Trine Immersion in Spain.—Gregory's Letter to Leander approving of One Immersion in Spain.—Maxentius of Aquila on Immersion.—The Catechism of the Council of Trent and Immersion.—Dr. Malcom describes a Catholic Immersion which he Witnessed in Milan.—Dean Stanley on Immersions in Milan.—The Baptistery of St. John de Lateran and its Immersions.—The Waxen Drawers anciently worn by Popes when Immersing.. 134

RUSSIA.

Vladimir the Great.—His Baptism.—The City of Kieff Immersed in the Dnieper.—Kelley, Dean Stanley, Mouravieff.—The Archdeacon's Story who Accompanied Macarius.—The Synod of Vladimir and Trine Immersion.—Kohl's account of a Russian Baptism which he Saw.—The Russian Dissenters Immerse.—Immersion of a Convert through a Hole in the Ice in 1869 in Russia... 155

CONTENTS.

TURKEY AND GREECE.—THE GREEK CHURCH.

The Constitution and Canons of the Holy Apostles.—Their Antiquity and Authority.—They Command Immersion. —Dionysius Exiguus, Strabo.—Gregory of Nyssa and Immersion. — Chrysostom, his Views of Baptism. — Philostorgius and Single and Trine Immersion.—Bayard Taylor describes a Baptism in Athens.—Dr. Arnold's Translation of the Greek Baptismal Service.— Dr. Arnold on Greek Immersion.—Dean Stanley on Greek Immersion.. 163

SERVIA.

Baptism of Prince Milan's Son.. 185

TURKEY, PERSIA, AND THE EAST.

A Miracle by Immersion.—Baptismal Service of the Nestorians now in Use.—The Armenians and Immersion.. 186

PALESTINE.

Jewish Proselyte Baptism.—Lightfoot.—A Modern Rabbi. —The New Testament and Immersion.—Lightfoot.— Jerome and Immersion.. 190

NORTH AFRICA.

Tertullian.—His Baptism is Immersion.—Tingo.—The Bishops of North Africa and Immersion.—Character of Augustine.—His Baptism.—Baptism of Epidophorus in Carthage.—Primasius of Adrumeta and Immersion. 196

EGYPT.

Boys Baptized by Athanasius.—Immersion among the Copts.. 206

ABYSSINIA.

Account of Immersions by Bruce............................ 209

CONCLUSION.

What has been Proved.—Thousands can be Immersed in One Day.—Probably a Majority of all Living and Dead Christians were Immersed.—Increase of the Baptist Denomination.—Immersionists will never yield.—Justification by Faith burst from under a Mountain of venerable Papal Heresies.—Immersion will arise from the Grave of Six Centuries..................................... 212

INDEX.. 217

THE
Baptism of the Ages and the Nations.

TRINE IMMERSION.

TRINE IMMERSION was the general practice of Christians from the end of the second till the close of the twelfth century. The proof of this statement is overwhelming. But the proof that triple immersion was the usual mode of baptism prevailing for a thousand years among Christians *begins* with Tertullian at the end of the second century, not with Christ. *Beyond Tertullian no record in the literature of men, in the book of God, or in any symbol known to mortals utters a single word about three immersions in baptism.* There is not the *faintest shadow* of evidence, before the close of the second century, that ever has been brought forward, or that can be secured, to prove the existence of trine immersion.

The impossibility of finding evidence for this practice before Tertullian's day is a deadly defect. If it only occupied a place in the Scriptures and in the observances of the inspired apostles, and perished immediately after the death of the beloved John, trine immersion could defy all opposition. But it is not in the "Book of books," where all Christ's institutions are described and recorded; the apostles, and the men who learned the truth directly from them, never even hint at it; and its advocates can only appeal to *conjectures* to establish its existence before the end of the second century. Jerome presents the truth about the origin of trine immersion when he says: "**Many** other things which are observed *by tradition* in the churches have secured the authority of *written law* for themselves, as, for example, *to immerse the head three times in the font.*"[1] No man that ever lived cherished an established religious practice like trine immersion more affectionately, and clung to it more tenaciously, than Jerome. No writer of the fourth century was better informed about the customs, present and past, of the Christian Church, than Jerome. And he was right; trine immersion was only a tradition, and of course ought to

[1] Multa alia quæ per traditionem in ecclesiis observantur, authoritatem sibi scriptæ legis usurpaverunt, velut in lavacro ter caput mergitare.—*Adver. Lucifereanos*, vol. iii. p. 63. Basil, Froben, 1516.

be rejected by all friends of *Bible* Christianity. Suppose that a vessel is near the shore in a fierce storm; the anchorage is excellent, and the ship has an anchor capable of saving her in any hurricane where it can secure a proper hold. The vessel carries a massive chain, whose huge links no power of the tempest can snap, and by this the anchor is bound to the ship. But half a dozen links next the anchor are gone, and some tarred rope, just strong enough to sustain the weight of the anchor whilst it is lowered into the sea, fastens the anchor to the great chain; and as soon as the fierce storm rages the rope breaks, the anchor is lost, and the ship is dashed to pieces on the rocks. The cable of history proving the long continuance of trine immersion stops with Tertullian; there is only the tarred rope of conjecture to reach from his day to Christ; and with Baptists that rope has given way long ago. As our fathers refused to receive infant baptism with nothing to support it but conjectures, so they rejected trine immersion resting on that poor basis; and their successors in the faith have followed their example.

ENGLAND,

AND THE PEOPLE WHO USE THE LANGUAGE OF BRITAIN.

St. Augustine Immersed Ten Thousand in the River Swale in a. d. 597.

WHEN the English first invaded Britain, their future home, they found its inhabitants a Christian people. The ancient Britons had been led to the Saviour by missionaries from the East, now unknown, in the first or second century; and long before the conquest of their country by "the Angles, Jutes, and Saxons" in the fifth century, the nation worshipped Jesus. The victorious English were fierce, persecuting Pagans. They burned the churches, tortured and murdered the clergy, and slew the people without mercy; and those who escaped their ferocious wrath had to fly for refuge to Cornwall and Wales. The new settlers reared temples in honor of their ancient gods all over Britain. In the end of the sixth century England was divided into several petty kingdoms by its heathen masters, the most powerful one of which, at that time, was Kent. The wife of Ethelbert, its king, was a French lady and an earnest Christian.

There is reason for believing that it was largely in response to her appeals that, in A. D. 596, Pope Gregory the Great sent forty missionaries into Kent with Augustine at their head. The preachers were so wonderfully successful that in a short time the whole people of Kent were professors of Christianity.

Ten Thousand Baptized on One Day.

Pope Gregory in a letter to Eulogius, Patriarch of Alexandria, informs him of this remarkable triumph. He writes: "More than ten thousand English, they tell us, were baptized by the same brother, our fellow-bishop [Augustine], which I communicate to you that you may know something to announce to the people of Alexandria, and that you may do something in prayer for the dwellers at the ends of the earth."[1]

The numbers baptized on this celebrated Christmas Day present no obstacle to our belief in the statement of Gregory. If the forty missionaries were engaged in baptizing, the ten thousand would only have furnished two hundred and fifty for each. But it is extremely probable that the converts baptized each other, while Augustine stood in some prominent place blessing the people and the waters.

[1] Plus quam decem millia Angli . . . sunt baptizati. *Gregor. Mag.*, tom. iii. lib. viii. Ep. 30., p. 952. Migne Parisiis, 1849.

Paulinus baptized several thousand on one baptismal occasion; Remigius enjoyed a similar blessing; and the apostles on the day of Pentecost were favored with an ingathering of three thousand.

THREE WITNESSES WHO GIVE TESTIMONY ABOUT THIS BAPTISM.

Dr. Thomas Fuller, a learned Episcopalian, in his *Church History* states[1] that "The archbishop [Augustine] is said to have commanded, by the voice of criers, *that the people should enter the river confidently*, two by two, and in the name of the Trinity baptize one another by turns." This was clearly a grand immersion.

Green's *History of the English People* is a recent work of great research and fidelity. Its Episcopalian author is "Examiner in the School of Modern History" in Oxford. In his history, Mr. Green writes: "As yet the results [of the labors of the Roman missionaries] were still distant. A year passed before even Ethelbert yielded, but from the moment of his conversion the new faith advanced rapidly. *The Kentish men crowded to baptism in the river Swale.* The under-kings of Essex and East Anglia received the

[1] Fuller's *Church History of Britain*, vol. i. pp. 97, 98. London, 1837.

creed of their over-lord."[1] The Swale spoken of by Green was in Kent. The Yorkshire Swale could not have been used for baptism until thirty years after the immersion of the ten thousand, as the people of that region were not converted till A. D. 627. With this fact Mr. Green is perfectly familiar. This river-baptism was an immersion.

Tradition bears strong testimony about this baptism. In an English almanac of recent date, on the lower half of one page, there is a record of the visit of Garibaldi to England, and of the birthdays of Prince Leopold, the Princess Beatrice, and George Canning; and then a statement that on the "*20th of April, A.D. 597, Ethelbert, King of Kent, and ten thousand Saxons were baptized in the river Swale.*" This is the uniform testimony of tradition, except about the day itself.

An intelligent gentleman of another denomination, now residing in Canterbury, in a private letter before me, after describing the river Swale, remarks: "*This is the Swale in Kent.* There is a river of the same name in Yorkshire, *but it was in the Swale in Kent, according to tradition, in which the baptism took place*" [of the ten thousand].

[1] Green's *History of the English People*, p. 55. New York, 1877.

The River Swale, in which the Ten Thousand were Baptized.

Ireland's *History of Kent* gives the following account of the Swale: "The stream which flows between the Isle of Sheppy and the mainland is called the Swale (Plate I.), and its two extremities the East and the West Swale. It extends for twelve miles, *and is navigable for ships of two hundred tons burthen.*" "The East Swale is nine miles from Canterbury." According to Ireland, the Swale was a river deep enough to be dangerous for ten thousand persons to throng its waters.

Gocelin's Account of the Baptism of the Ten Thousand.

This monk is called Joscelyn by William of Malmesbury, Gotzelin by Dupin, and Gocelin by the *Patrologiæ Latinæ*. He was a Frenchman by birth, and he came to England in the eleventh century. He was familiar with the *Chronicles of Kent—written long before his day—*"two of which were collated by him."[1] William of Malmesbury tells us[2] that he was regarded as a man "of un-

---

[1] Bede's *Ecclesiastical History*, p. 37, preface. Bohn, London, 1870.

[2] *English Chronicle*, lib. iv. cap. i. p. 355. London, 1847.

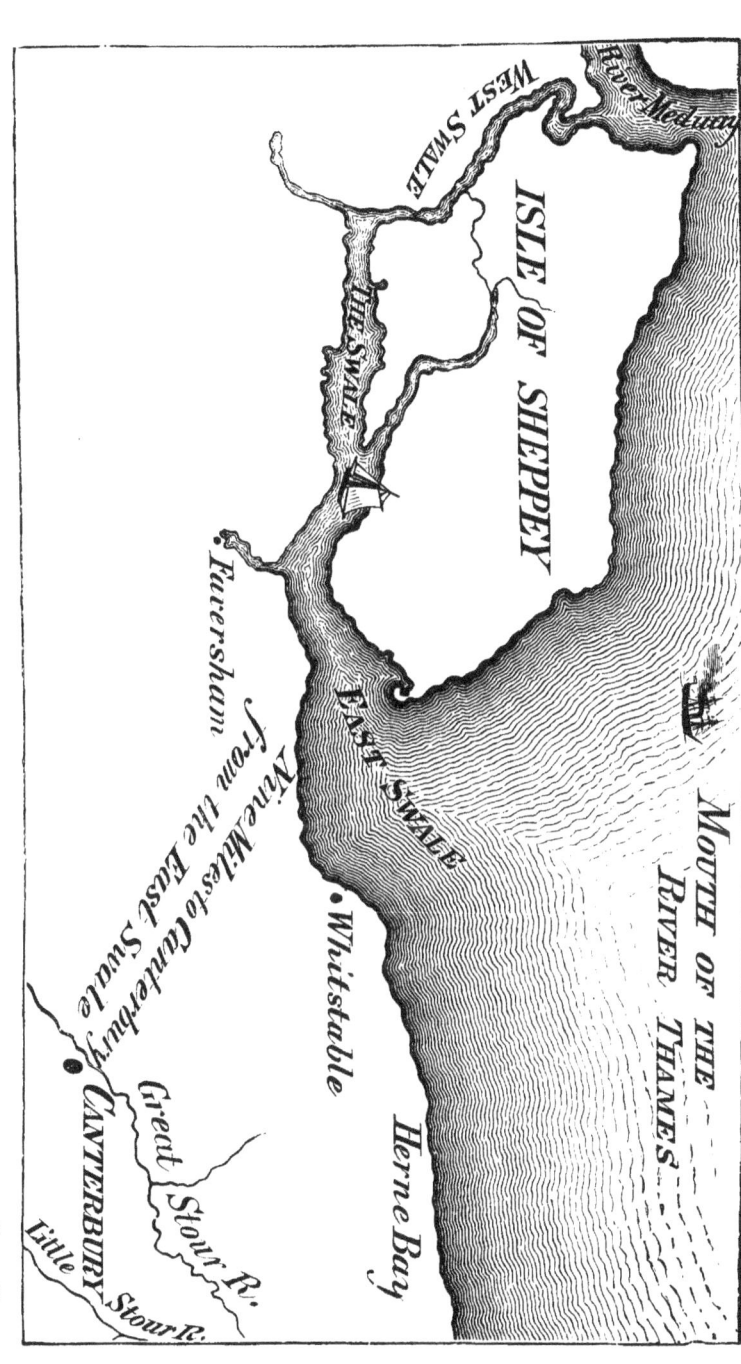

RIVER SWALE IN KENT.

common learning" and of great worth. In his *Life of St. Augustine* he speaks of him—

"As rejoicing in success, as men delight in the harvest, and as conquerors exult in the spoils they have captured. He secured," says he, "on all sides large numbers for Christ, so that on that birthday of the Lord, celebrated by the melodious anthems of all heaven, more than ten thousand of the English were born again *in the laver of holy baptism, with an infinite number of women and children, in a river which the English call Sirarios, the Swale, as if at one birth of the Church, and from one womb.*

"These persons, at the command of the divine teacher, as if he were an angel from heaven calling upon them, *all entered the dangerous depth of the river, two and two together, as if it had been a solid plain;* and in the true faith, confessing the exalted Trinity, they were baptized one by the other in turns, the apostolic leader blessing the water. . . . So great a progeny for heaven *born out of a deep whirlpool!*"[1]

[1] "In fluvio qui Sirarios Anglice dicitur, . . . omnes pariter bini et bini, minacem fluminis profunditatem, ac si solidum campum ingrediuntur . . . alter ab altero. . . . Tanta progenies in cœlum de profundo gurgite nasceretur." *Vita Sanct. August., Patrologiæ Latinæ*, vol. 80, pp. 79, 80. Migne. Parisiis.

The word "whirlpool" is a striking figure of the chasm made in the waters by plunging the candidate under their surface, and of the returning waters as they rush together over the immersed body.

Gocelin, like many others, in his *Life of Augustine* makes the mistake of giving to the Swale of Yorkshire the credit which was due to the Swale of Kent; but this is a matter of no moment, and a very natural mistake in a foreigner.

Gocelin had the original *Chronicles of Kent*, centuries old in his day; and when he describes these throngs as "*baptized in the river Swale,*" as having "*entered the dangerous depth of the river,*" and as being "*born for heaven* [baptized] *out of a deep whirlpool,*" the evidence of their immersion is overwhelming.

We might refer to the universal practice of immersion throughout the whole Christian communities on earth in the sixth century as evidence that Augustine would be likely to follow the custom of all other churches in his mode of baptism. We might point to the fact that Pope Gregory sent him to England; that the pontiff exercised over him the authority of a spiritual director; and that he received from him unquestioning obedience. Bede[1] has a list of queries sent by Augustine to Gregory,

---

[1] Bædæ, *Hist. Eccles.*, i. 27, p. 46. Oxonii, 1846.

with the answers returned by the pope, which prove that after Augustine's consecration to the see of Canterbury he administered the entire affairs of his new office, even in insignificant matters, according to the wishes of his master at Rome. And as Gregory wrote, at this very time, about the baptismal usages of Rome and Italy, "We immerse three times,"[1] we might establish a moral certainty that Augustine immersed three times. We might exhibit the convincing evidence that the English Church immersed her members *for nine hundred years after Augustine's death*, and we might naturally infer that she only followed the instructions and example of her founder Augustine; but it is needless. The testimony already given renders it certain that the first great baptism of "more than ten thousand of the English" in Kent was by immersion.

This was the first baptism in that race which owns the British Islands, and India, and territories and fleets all over the lands and the oceans of the globe —a race that has reared this glorious republic, colossal in resources, in area, and in mental, moral, and material powers—a race that exerts the greatest influence over the nations of the earth of any

[1] Tertio mergimus. *Patrologiæ Latinæ*, vol. 77, p. 497. Migne. Parisiis.

kindred peoples in human history—and a race that was snatched from barbarism, poverty, and insignificance by the religion of Jesus, and by his gospel invested with all its spiritual and temporal glories. In view of these considerations Augustine's baptism in the Swale is one of the most important events in the annals of mankind.

Paulinus Baptizes Edwin, King of Northumbria, at York, with Many of his People, in a. d. 627.

Alcuin relates that "Easter having come, when the king had decided to be baptized with his people under the lofty walls of York, in which, by his orders, a little house [of wood, according to Bede] was quickly erected for God, that under its roof he might receive the sacred water of baptism. During the sunshine of that festive and holy day he was dedicated to Christ *in the saving fountain*,[1] with his family and nobles, and with the common people following. . . . York remained illustrious, distinguished with great honor, because in that sacred place King Edwin *was washed in the water*" [of baptism].

Dr. Giles, in a note in his translation of Bede's

---

[1] Fonte salutifero . . . fuit lavatus in unda. *Alcuini Carmina, Patrol. Lat.*, vol. 101, p. 818. Migne. Parisiis.

Ecclesiastical History, states that "parts of the original wooden structure of King Edwin were discovered in making repairs in the present cathedral of York." And he refers to Brown's *History of St. Peter's Church of York* [the cathedral], which in Plate III. shows "the probable position of the wooden baptistery *enclosing a spring still remaining.*"[1]

Edwin, his family, his nobles, and the common people, probably numbering several thousand, "were dedicated to Christ *in the saving fountain,*" "*were washed in the water;*" and the Episcopalian translator of Bede's *Ecclesiastical History* makes himself responsible for a statement that the spring is in the cathedral of York to-day, in which, probably, this vast immersion took place. This was the first triumph of Christianity in the north of England. It occurred A. D. 627.

Three Thousand were Baptized by Paulinus in Northumberland at Easter, A. D. 627.

About eleven miles from the Cheviot Hills, which separate England from Scotland, and about the same distance from Alnwick Castle, the well-known residence of the dukes of Northumberland, and two miles from the village of Harbottle, there is a re-

[1] Bede's *Ecclesiastical History* p. 97. Bohn, London, 1870.

markable fountain. It issues forth from the top of a slight elevation, or little hill. It has at present as its basin a cavity about thirty-four feet long, twenty feet wide, and two feet deep. By placing a board over a small opening at one end, its depth can be considerably increased. A stream flows from it, which forms a little creek. A few shade trees with knife-marks, and benches similarly adorned, bear witness to the presence of visitors. Indeed, the spring is a place of public resort for the population for many miles around, and for numerous strangers, on account of its early baptismal associations. The author of this little work in the August of 1869, during the half hour which he spent beside this beautiful fountain, saw several small parties of visitors who had come to examine "The Lady's Well," as it is called,—that is, undoubtedly, "Our Lady's Well," the Virgin Mary's Well.

An ancient statue, as large as life, lay prostrate in the fountain for ages—probably from the period when the monasteries were destroyed in the time of Henry VIII. This statue, when the writer saw it, was leaning against a tree at the fountain. It was most likely the statue of Paulinus. It was called "the bishop." Its drapery, the action of the atmosphere upon the stone of which it is made, and its general appearance show that it was set up at a very remote period, perhaps two or three centuries after Paulinus baptized the Northumbrian multitude in the fountain.

The traditions of Northumberland point out the Lady's Well as one of the baptisteries of Paulinus, the apostle of the north of England. *The History of Northumberland* confirms its traditions. A large crucifix was standing in the centre of the fountain in 1869 (Plate II.), erected under the superintendence of the Episcopal Vicar of Harbottle—a worthy clergyman, a graduate of Oxford, then living. On one side of the base of the crucifix it bears the following inscription: "In this place Paulinus, the bishop, baptized three thousand Northumbrians, Easter, 627."

The learned Camden, whose authority on such a question is universally respected by those competent to judge, speaks of "Harbottle on the Coquet River, near to which is Holystone, where it is said that Paulinus, when the Church of the English was first planted, baptized many thousands of men."[1] Camden was born in 1551, and the tradition about the bap

---

[1] Harbottle, cui contiguum est Holyston . . . ubi in primitiva Anglorum ecclesia Paulinum multa hominum millia baptizasse fama obtinet. Guili. Camdeni, *Britannia*, p. 365. Amsterdami, 1639.

tism rested upon a strong foundation, or he would not have inserted it in his celebrated *Britannia*.

The village of Holystone is almost within call of the "Lady's Well." A nunnery stood for ages in this village, to which the fountain belonged, and which was most probably built there to commemorate the sanctity and to appropriate the efficacy of so holy a font; and its existence is strong corroborative evidence of the sacred use to which the pure waters of the fountain were devoted by Paulinus. Some scanty remains of the convent are still to be seen in Holystone.

More Great Baptisms in the North of England.

Bede, the father of English history, was one of the purest and best men that ever lived. He was a prolific writer on several important subjects; and though he died in A. D. 735, a new edition of his entire works in five volumes has been issued in Paris within twenty years. Treating of the conversion of his Northumbrian fathers in England, in A. D. 627, he says:

"Paulinus, coming with the king and queen of the Northumbrians to the royal country-seat of Adgefrin,[1] stayed there with them *thirty-six days*,

[1] Yeverin in Glendale, near Wooler, in Northumberland.

fully occupied in catechising and baptizing; during which days, from morning till night, he did nothing else but instruct the people resorting from all the villages and places, in Christ's saving word; and when instructed, *they were washed in the river Glen,*[1] which was near by, with the water of absolution."[2] He adds: "These things happened in the province of the Bernicians; but in that of the Deiri also, where he was accustomed often to be with the king, *he baptized in the river Swale,*[3] *which flows past* the village of Cataract."[4] Bede records

The Baptism of a Multitude.

He speaks of an old man who said that "*he and a great multitude*[5] *were baptized at noonday, in the presence of King Edwin, in the river Trent,* by the bishop Paulinus, near the city which in the English tongue is called Tiovulfingacestir."[6] These baptisms *in rivers* were surely immersions. The places where

[1] The river Bowent.

[2] Fluvio Gleni . . . lavacro remissionis abluere. *Hist. Eccles.*, lib. ii. 14, p. 104. Oxonii, 1846.

[3] Baptizabat in Sualo fluvio . . . praterfluit. *Ibid.*

[4] Carrick, Yorkshire.

[5] Baptizatum se fuisse . . . et multam populi turbam in fluvio Treenta. *Ibid.*, ii. 16, p. 107. Oxonii, 1846.

[6] Southwell, Nottinghamshire.

the ordinance was administered show the *mode* clearly enough. Then Paulinus was a missionary from Rome, where, according to a letter of Gregory the Great to Leander, they practised trine immersion.

BAPTISM OF THE MERCIANS, A POWERFUL SAXON KINGDOM IN ENGLAND.

Alcuin states that after the death of Penda, the fierce heathen king of the Mercians, their sovereign, Osway, "*caused them to be washed in the consecrated river of baptism.*"[1] This occurred about A. D. 658. Baptism in England at first was administered in fountains and rivers, until baptisteries were erected.

CAEDWALLA, KING OF THE WEST SAXONS, IS IMMERSED AT ROME.

This ferocious tyrant shed blood as if it was worth less than water, and, finding death drawing near, he resolved to go to Rome in A. D. 689 and wash away his sins in baptism; and if possible he wanted to die soon after. Alcuin tells us that he passed over the ocean and the Alps, and entered Rome, where his presence gave delight to its courteous citizens, and special joy to the clergy; " Whilst

[1] Sacrato faciens baptismatis amne lavare. *Patrol. Lat.*, vol. 101, p. 824. Migne. Parisiis.

the happy king," he declares, "was deemed worthy *to be immersed in the whirlpool of baptism.*"[1]

The word "whirlpool," as noticed elsewhere, describes the chasm made in the waters by the body of the baptized person as he sinks in them, and the rushing of the waters to cover the candidate for immersion.

The Venerable Bede and Immersion.

Bede, whom Catholics and Protestants unite in regarding as a faithful servant of Jesus Christ—the first great English author who appeared in the new country of the "Angles and Jutes and Saxons," a man of vast information for his times, and of religious knowledge which is a treasure to-day—writes these words about baptism:

"For he truly who is baptized *is seen to descend into the fountain—he is seen to be dipped in the waters—he is seen to ascend from the waters;* but that which makes the font regenerate him can by no means be seen. The piety of the faithful alone perceives that a sinner *descends into the font*, and a cleansed man ascends [from it]; a son of death descends [into it], but a son of the resurrection ascends

---

[1] Mergi meruit baptismi gurgite. *Patrol. Lat.*, vol. 101, p. 1310. Migne. Parisiis.

[from it]; a son of treachery descends [into it], but a son of reconciliation ascends [from it]; a son of wrath descends [into it], but a son of compassion ascends [from it]; a son of the devil descends [into it], but a son of God ascends [from it]."[1]

Bede, the father of English history, who died A. D. 735, had no conception of any baptism which did not require a descent into the font—an immersion in its waters, and an ascent out of those waters.

The Council of Celichyth, held in England in A. D. 816, on Baptism.

The second canon of this council reads: "Let the presbyters know when they administer sacred baptism, *not to pour holy water upon the heads of the infants, but always to immerse them in the laver, after the example given by the Son of God himself to every believer when he was three times immersed in the waters of the Jordan.*"[2] Whilst at this period, either in or

[1] Nam videter quidem, qui baptizatur, in fontem descendere, videtur aquis intingi, videtur de aquis ascendere . . . peccator in fontem descendet, sed purificatus ascendit. . . . Bæda Ven., in *St. Joannis, Evang. Expos.*, iii. 5, vol. 92, pp. 668, 669; *Patrol. Lat.* Migne. Parisiis.

[2] Ut non effundant aquam sanctam super capita infantium sed semper mergantur in lavacro . . . quando esset ter mersus in undis Jordanis. *Can. II. Conc. Celich., Hardu, Conc. Collec.*, vol. iv. p. 1224. Parisiis, 1715.

out of England, the question of pouring in baptism was evidently agitated, the decision of the British bishops plainly showed that in their judgment pouring was the destruction of the truth. This canon is recorded by Harduin, another learned Jesuit, in his standard work *Conciliorum Collectio*.

FRIDEGOD AND IMMERSION.

Fridegod was a monk of Canterbury in the tenth century, who, at the request of Odo, his archbishop, composed lives of St. Wilfred and St. Owen in verse. In his *Life of St. Wilfred* he states that "he showed that those to be saved should *be immersed in the clear waters*." Elsewhere he asserts that the "common people seeking *holy baptism are immersed*." [1]

KING ETHELRED'S IMMERSION.

William of Malmesbury, an author whose veracity and care have been deservedly commended, declares that "when the little boy [Ethelred] *was immersed in the font of baptism*, the bishops standing around, the sacrament was marred by a sad accident which made St. Dunstan utter an unfavorable prophecy." [2]

---

[1] Liquidis salvandos tinguere . . . tinguntur plebes sanctum baptisma petentes. *Fridey., De Vita St. Wilfr., Patrol. Lat.*, vol. 133, pp. 993, 1003.

[2] Cum pusiolus in fontem baptismi mergeretur circumstanti-

Ethelred ascended the throne A. D. 979, and reigned for thirty years.

The font, a picture of which we give (Plate III.), is now in the church of St. Martin, Canterbury, England. The church is very small and of great age. *The Canterbury Guide* of this year says that "the quantity of Roman bricks which may be detected in many parts of the structure would indicate that it was originally a Roman building. The walls of the chancel are almost entirely of Roman brick."[1] The same *Guide* says: "The font is certainly one of the first in England. It has no stand, but rests on the ground. It is about three feet in height, *and capacious within.* The sculptures upon it are a sort of ornamental interlacing in low relief." In a private letter from a courteous gentleman in Canterbury, who recently measured the font for me, he states that "the font itself is very ancient. It is thirty-eight inches high, twenty-nine inches deep [the cavity], thirty-three inches wide [evidently the diameter including rim]. The rim is five and a quarter inches thick. The inside is lined with lead, which, of course, is *not so old as the font itself;* and

bus episcopis, alvi profluvio sacramenta interpolavit. *Willelmi Malmb., Gesta. Reg. Angl.*, cap. ii. 164. *Patrol. Lat.*, vol. 179, p. 1131. Migne. Parisiis.

[1] *The New Illustrated Canterbury Guide*, p. 31.

Baptism of the Ages.

FONT IN CHURCH OF ST. MARTIN, CANTERBURY.

the depth, as it is now used with this lining, forms a sort of basin which is only thirteen inches. The font is circular in shape."

From this letter we learn that the *original cavity of the font,* before the introduction of the leaden lining, was *twenty-nine inches deep and twenty-two and a half inches wide.* In such a font Ethelred was baptized by immersion, the only form of baptism practised in England till after the Reformation. And it was intended to accommodate persons of some growth as well as infants.

ANLAF, KING OF THE NORWEGIANS, IS IMMERSED IN ENGLAND.

Roger of Wendover wrote a work which he called *The Flowers of History,* relating the history of England from A. D. 449 to A. D. 1235. The following is from the translation of that work by Dr. J. A. Giles, late fellow of Corpus Christi College, Oxford, an Episcopalian:

"Sweyn, king of the Danes, and Anlaf, king of the Norwegians, arrived at London with ninety-four cogues on the nativity of the blessed Mary, and made a fierce assault with a view to take it; but being repulsed with great loss by the citizens, they turned their rage against the provinces. King Ethelred thereupon, with the advice of his nobles, made them a payment of sixteen thousand pounds, collected from the whole of England, to induce them to cease from robbing and slaughtering the innocent people. King Ethelred at this time despatched Elfege, Bishop of Winchester, and Duke Athelwold to King Anlaf, whom they brought in peace to the royal vill where King Ethelred then was, *and at his request dipped him in the sacred font,* after which he was confirmed by the bishop, the king adopting him as his son, and honoring him with royal presents; and the following summer he returned to his own country in peace."[1]

Many of these Scandinavian royal pirates were baptized after wholesale robberies and murders in the British Islands and in France, but the ordinance was shockingly profaned by its application to such impenitent enemies of the human race.

Lanfranc and Immersion.

Lanfranc was an Italian who reached England by way of Normandy, where he was abbot of the famous monastery of Bec. As an instructor at Bec his reputation spread over a large part of Europe, and drew throngs of students to the abbey schools. He enjoyed the confidence of William the Conqueror, who made him Archbishop of Canter-

[1] *Flowers of History,* at A. D. 994, p. 272. London, 1849.

bury four years after the victory of Hastings had placed the crown of England on his head. His reputation was greatly increased by his *Exposition of the Epistles of Paul.* Commenting on Philippians iii. 20, he says:

"*For as Christ lay three days in the sepulchre, so in baptism let there be a trine immersion.*"[1] This was the testimony of a native Italian, a great French teacher and the head of the English Church.

Cardinal Pullus on Immersion.

This cultivated Englishman occupied a very prominent place in theological and general learning. He read lectures for five years in Oxford, and afterward he was professor of divinity in Paris. He resided for a considerable period in Rome, where he was such a favorite with the pope that he was created a cardinal in A. D. 1144.

In his only work which has come down to us, a valuable system of divinity, he writes of baptism:

"Whilst the candidate for baptism in water *is immersed the death of Christ is suggested; whilst immersed, and covered with water, the burial of Christ is shown forth; whilst he is raised from the waters, the*

---

[1] Ut enim tribus diebus jacuit Christus in sepulchro, sic in baptismate trina sit immersio. Vol. 150, p. 315; *Patrol. Lat.* Migne. Parisiis.

resurrection of Christ is proclaimed. The immersion is repeated three times, out of reverence for the Trinity and on account of the three days' burial of Christ. In the burial of the Lord the day follows the night three times; *in baptism also trine emersion accompanies trine immersion.*"[1] The most beautiful exposition of Rom. vi. 4 ever penned!

The Christening of Prince Arthur and of the Princess Margaret.

Arthur was the oldest son of Henry VII., King of England, and the brother of Henry VIII., first the persecutor of the Reformation and then its protector. Arthur was born A. D. 1486. He married Catharine of Aragon, who after his death became the wife of Henry VIII. and the mother of the bloody Queen Mary. Leland, whose authority in such a matter is unquestionable, says, in a very lengthy account of Arthur's baptism: "The body of all the cathedral church of Winchester was hung with cloth of arras, and in the middle, beside the font of the said

---

[1] Dum baptizandus aquæ immergitur, mors Christi insinuatur; dum sub aqua latet mersus, sepultura Christi repræsentatur; dum sublevatur ex aquis, resurrectio Christi declaratur. Mersio repetitur tertio . . . in baptismo quoque trinam trina mersionem emersio comitatur. Card. Rob. Pull., lib. oct.; *Patrol. Lat.,* vol. 186, p. 843.

church, was ordained and prepared a solemn font[1] in manner and form as ensueth. First, there was ordained in manner of a stage of seven steps, square or round like, an high cross covered with red worsted, and up in the midst a post made of iron to bear the font of silver gilt, which *within* side was well dressed [lined] with fine linen cloth [to protect the babe from touching the cold stone or metal], and near the same on the west side was a step, like a block, for the bishop to stand on, covered also with red saye; and over the front, of a good height, a rich canopy with a great gilt ball, lined and fringed without curtains. On the north side was ordained a travers hung with cloth of arras, and upon the one side thereof, within side, another travers of red sarsnet. There was fire without fumigations, ready against the prince's coming. And without, the steps of said font were railed with good timber. . . . And Queen Elisabeth was in the church abiding the coming of the prince. . . . Incontinent [immediately] *after the prince was put into the font* the officers-at-arms put on their coats, and all their torches were lighted."[2] Here the baptism was by dipping in the font.

[1] A new font was commonly made for the baptism of a royal child.

[2] *Lelandi Collectanea*, vol. iv. pp. 204–206. London, 1774

The Baptism of Arthur's Sister.

Margaret was baptized in 1490. When very young, in 1502, she was married to James IV., King of Scotland. She was the grandmother of Mary, Queen of Scots, and aunt of Queen Elisabeth. Writing of her baptism, Leland says: "On the morning of her baptism the aforesaid newborn princess was christened in the following manner: The rich font of Canterbury and Westminster Church was prepared, as of old time the custom was for kings' children, with a rich round canopy. with a great gilt ball. The aforesaid princess was brought from the queen's chamber into the White Hall, borne by the Marchioness of Berkeley; and to her gave assistance the Earls of Arundel and Shrewsbury. My Lady Anne, the queen's sister, bore next before her the chrism, with a marvellous rich cross lace; and before her the Viscount Wellis bore a rich salt of gold garnished with precious stones; and before him the Earl of Essex bore a taper. . . . When the said princess was brought to the porch of Westminster Church, the Lord John Alcock, Bishop of Ely, was there ready in pontificals, who christened the princess. *As soon as she was put into the font* all the torches were lighted. . . . "[1] I have given but a small part of this

[1] *Lelandi Collectanea*, vol. iv. pp. 253, 254. London, 1774.

royal Romish christening as treasured up by Leland, but I have quoted enough to show that the little princess was put into the font instead of being sprinkled with water. In Leland there are substantially the same accounts given of the baptisms of Edward VI. and Queen Elizabeth.

In the reign of Edward VI., Walker, a very high authority on baptismal customs, says: "*Dipping was at this time the more usual*, but sprinkling was *sometimes* used."[1] These times were probably still times of real weakness.

IMMERSION IN ENGLAND IN THE REIGN O "BLOODY MARY."

Watson, Bishop of Lincoln, in 1558 published a volume of sermons, in one of which he says:

"Though *the old and ancient tradition of the Church hath been from the beginning to dip the child three times*, etc., yet that is not of such necessity; but that *if he be but once dipped in the water, it is sufficient*. Yea, and in time of *great peril and necessity*, if the water be but poured on his head, it will suffice."[2]

---

[1] Walker's *Doctrine of Baptisms*, chap. x. p. 147. London, 1678.

[2] *Holsome and Catholyke Doctryne Concerninge the Seven Sacraments*, pp. 22, 23. London, 1558.

Immersion in England in 1644.

The Rev. Thomas Blake, living in Tamworth in Staffordshire, in 1644, writes of immersion:

"I have been *an eye-witness of many infants dipped*, and I know it to have been *the constant practice of many ministers in their places for many years together.*"[1]

Mr. Blake practised infant baptism, and had no sympathy with the people who rejected it.

Immersion in the Westminster Assembly of Divines.

This great council of godly men framed the Confession of Faith still received by all Scotch Presbyterians, by all Scotch-Irish and English Presbyterians, and by the great majority of American Presbyterians—a Confession held in high esteem by many Baptists and others.

Neal, the historian of the English Puritans, declares that "there was not one professed Anabaptist in this Assembly."[2] It is remarkable, under these circumstances, that any member of it should advocate dipping, if immersion had not been a common custom of all Christians a few ages before. Dr.

---

[1] *The Birth Privilege*, etc., by Thomas Blake, A. M., p. 33. London, 1644.

[2] Neal's *History of the Puritans*, iii. 116. Dublin, 1755.

John Lightfoot, one of the ablest members of the Assembly, kept a journal of the proceedings of that body, and he says that on August 7th, 1644—

"Then fell we upon the work of the day, which was about baptizing of the child, whether to dip or sprinkle him; and this proposition, 'It is lawful and sufficient to besprinkle the child,' had been canvassed before our adjourning, and was ready now to vote. But I spoke against it, as being very unfit to vote that it is lawful to sprinkle when every one grants it. Whereupon it was fallen upon, sprinkling being granted, whether dipping should be tolerated with it. And here fell we upon a large and long discourse, whether *dipping were essential, or used in the first institution,* or in the Jews' custom. Mr. Coleman went about in a large discourse to prove *tauveleh* [Hebrew for dipping] to be dipping over head, which I answered at large. . . . After a long dispute it was at last put to the question whether the *Directory* [for Worship] should run, 'The minister shall take water and sprinkle or pour it with his hand upon the face or forehead of the child;' and it was voted so indifferently that we were glad to count names twice; *for so many were unwilling to have dipping excluded that the vote came to an equality within one; for the one side was twenty-four, the other twenty-five*—the twenty-four for the reserving of dipping, and the twenty-five against it. *And then grew a great heat upon it; and when we had done all, we concluded upon nothing in it;* but the business was recommitted." The next day, in opposition to the friends of the primitive mode of baptism—of whom Mr. Marshall on the second day was the principal leader—it was decided that the *Directory* should read, " He is to baptize the child with water, which for the manner of doing is not only lawful, but also sufficient and most expedient, to be by pouring or sprinkling water on the face of the child, without any other ceremony." [1] This was a singular discussion in the venerable Assembly that framed the great Presbyterian Confession of Faith. To-day our Presbyterian brethren in general regard immersion with an honest, manly hatred, and a hatred that considerably exceeds the repugnance shown by any other religious community. Mr. Coleman was " so perfect a master of the Hebrew language that he was commonly called Rabbi Coleman;" and when he died " the whole Assembly did him the honor to attend his funeral in a body, March 30, 1646." [2]

Mr. Marshall was a great favorite with the Long

[1] *The Whole Works of Lightfoot,* vol. xiii. 300, 301. London, 1824.

[2] Neal's *History of the Puritans,* iii. 294. Dublin, 1755.

Parliament, before which he often preached, and it was accustomed to ask his opinions on all questions relating to religion. He was employed in most, if not in all, the treaties between the king and Parliament. A bitter enemy spoke of him as "a famous incendiary and assistant to the Parliamentarians; their trumpet in their fasts, their confessor in their sickness, their counselor in their assemblies, their chaplain in their treaties, and their champion in their disputations."[1]

"ANNOTATIONS OF THE [WESTMINSTER] ASSEMBLY OF DIVINES" ON BAPTISM.

On Romans vi. 4 this valuable commentary says: "Buried with Him by baptism. In this phrase the apostle seemeth to allude to the ancient manner of baptism, *which was to dip the parties baptized, and as it were bury them under the water for a while, and then to draw them out of it and lift them up, to represent the burial of our old man and our resurrection to newness of life.*"[2] The authors of this commentary undoubtedly believed that Paul's baptism was immersion.

It is denied that the Westminster Assembly ever authorized or approved of this commentary. It is admitted, however, by very respectable authority that the Parliament which created the Assembly

[1] Neal's *History of the Puritans*, iv. p. 130.
[2] Rom. vi. 4. London edition, 1651.

by one of its committees named the commentators and furnished them with books, and that seven of the committee of eleven persons who prepared the work were members of the Westminster Assembly of Divines.[1]

The great Dr. Chalmers of the Free Church of Scotland agreed with the exposition of Romans vi. 3-7 given in *The Annotations of the Assembly of Divines*. Commenting on that passage, he says:

"*The original meaning of the word 'baptism' is 'immersion;'* and though we regard it as a matter of indifference whether the ordinance be performed in this way or by sprinkling, yet *we doubt not that the prevalent style of the administration in the apostles' days was by an actual submersion of the whole body under water*. We advert to this for the purpose of throwing light on the analogy that is instituted in these verses."[2]

Dr. Chalmers in this quotation places himself with the great Church Fathers, and ecclesiastical historians of all ages, as to the original mode of baptism, and with the Baptists of every land.

Dr. William Cave on Immersion.

Cave was born A. D. 1634 in England. He was

[1] Neal's *History of the Puritans*, pp. 386, 387. Dublin, 1755.
[2] Chalmers's works, *Commentary on Romans*, at vi. 4.

educated at the University of Cambridge, and he lived and died an Episcopalian. Cave's *Primitive Christianity* is a work of great learning, rare merit, and commendable candor. It has come down to our times in recent editions. The copy before me was published at Oxford, in 1840, and no doubt it will journey down the ages in other editions for generations to come. Treating of baptism, he writes:

"Their *baptisteria,* or fonts as we call them, were usually *very large and capacious,* not only that they might comport with the general customs of those times [the times of the early Christians] of persons baptized *being immersed or put under water,* but because the stated times of baptism, returning so seldom, great multitudes were usually baptized at the same time. In the middle of the font there was a partition, the one part for men, the other for women, that to avoid offence and scandal they might be baptized asunder." . . . "The party to be baptized was *wholly immerged, or put under water, which was almost the constant and universal custom of those times,* whereby they did more notably and significantly express the three great ends and effects of baptism; *for as in immersion there are, in a manner, three several acts—the putting the person into water, his abiding there for a little time, and his rising up again*—so by these were represented Christ's death, burial, and resurrection; and in conformity thereunto our dying unto sin, the destruction of its power, and our resurrection to a new course of life. By the persons being put into water was lively represented the putting off the body of the sins of the flesh, and being washed from the filth and pollution of them; *by his abode under it*—which was *a kind of burial in the water*—his entering into a state of death or mortification, like as Christ remained for some time under the state or power of death; therefore, ' as many as are baptized into Christ' are said ' to be baptized into his death, and to be buried with him by baptism into death,' that, the old man being crucified with him, the body of sin might be destroyed, that henceforth he might not serve sin, for he that is dead is freed from sin, as the apostle clearly explains the meaning of the rite; and then by *his emersion, or rising up out of the water*, was signified his entering upon a new course of life, differing from that which he lived before; ' that like as Christ was raised up from the dead by the glory of the Father, even so we also should walk in newness of life.' " [1]

" This immersion was performed thrice, the person baptized being three several times *put under water.*" The authority of Dr. William Cave for an ancient

[1] Cave's *Primitive Christianity*, pp. 152, 155–157. Oxford, 1840.

Christian custom will seldom be questioned by persons competent to judge.

THE REV. WILLIAM WALL, A. M., VICAR OF SHOREHAM, KENT, ENGLAND, ON IMMERSION.

Mr. Wall was an eminent scholar. His *History of Infant Baptism* is a work of very great merit; and though we dissent from its main conclusion, yet its hearty endorsement of immersion makes it a welcome witness for that truth.

On the 9th of February, 1705, *he received the thanks of the Convocation of the English Church for his learned book.* This was a very unusual compliment, and at the time there were men of great learning in that ancient ecclesiastical parliament. In his erudite work, Wall states that "their general and ordinary way was to *baptize by immersion, or dipping the person, whether it were an infant or grown man or woman, into the water.* This is so plain and clear by an infinite number of passages, that as one cannot but pity the weak endeavors of such Pedobaptists as would maintain the negative of it, so also we ought to disown and show a dislike of the *profane scoffs* which some people give to the English Antipedobaptists [Baptists] merely for the use of dipping. It is one thing to maintain that that circumstance is not absolutely necessary to the essence of baptism, and another to go about and represent it as ridiculous and foolish, or as shameful and indecent, *when it was in all probability the way by which our blessed Saviour, and for certain was the most usual and ordinary way by which the ancient Christians, did receive their baptism."* [1]

"The Greek Church, in all the branches of it, does still use immersion, and they hardly count a child, except in case of sickness, well baptized without it. *And so do all other Christians in the world except the Latins.* That which I hinted at before is a rule that does not fail in any particular that I know of: *All those nations of Christians that do now or formerly did submit to the authority of the Bishop of Rome do ordinarily baptize their infants by pouring or sprinkling.* And though the English did not receive this custom *till after the decay of Popery*, yet they have since received it from such neighbor nations as had begun it in the times of the pope's power. *But all the other Christians who never owned the pope's usurped power do and ever did dip their infants in the ordinary use.*

"And if we take the division of the world from the three main parts of it, all the Christians in Asia, all in Africa, and about one-third part of Europe,

[1] Wall's *History of Infant Baptism*, p. 706. Nashville, 1860.

AGES AND THE NATIONS. 53

are of the last sort [immersionists]; in which third part of Europe are comprehended the Christians of Græcia, Thracia, Servia, Bulgaria, Rascia, Wallachia, Moldavia, Russia, Nigra, etc., and even the Muscovites, who, if coldness of the country will excuse, might plead for a dispensation with the most reason of any."[1] Wall gives excellent testimony for the Baptists, though an Episcopalian.

THE MANUAL FOR THE USE OF SARUM, AND IMMERSION.

This was a document of great authority in England, and it was occasionally quoted on the European continent. Speaking of it, Wall says: "The offices or liturgies for public baptism in the Church of England, so far as I can learn, did all along *enjoin dipping, without any mention of pouring or sprinkling.* The *Manuale ad usum Sarum,* printed 1530, the twenty-first of Henry VIII., orders thus for the public baptisms: Then let the priest take the child, and having asked the name, *baptize him by dipping him in the water thrice,* etc. And John Frith, writing in the year 1533 a treatise of baptism, calls the outward part of it '*the plunging down in the water and lifting up again,*' which he

[1] Wall's *History of Infant Baptism,* pp. 727, 728. Nashville, 1860.

5*

often mentions without ever speaking of **pouring or sprinkling.**"[1]

JOSEPH BINGHAM AND THE BAPTISM OF THE PRIMITIVE CHURCH.

Bingham was a learned Episcopalian. His *Antiquities of the Christian Church* for more than one hundred and fifty years has enjoyed the unbounded admiration of students of primitive church history of all countries and communities.

It contains a larger amount of exact scholarly in formation about the doctrines and practices of the early Christians and errorists than any work ever written. Of baptism Bingham says:

"*Persons were usually baptized by immersion, or dipping of their whole bodies under water*, to represent the death, burial, and resurrection of Christ together, and therewith to signify their own dying unto sin, the destruction of its power, and their resurrection to a new life. There are a great many passages in the Epistles of St. Paul which plainly refer to this custom. Rom vi. 4: 'We are buried with him by baptism into death, that like as Christ was raised up from the dead by the glory of the Father, even so we also should walk in new-

[1] Wall's *History of Infant Baptism*, pp. 715, 716. Nashville, 1860.

ness of life.' So again, Col. iii. 12: 'Buried with him in baptism, wherein ye are also risen with him, through the faith of the operation of God, who raised him from the dead.' And as this was the original apostolical practice, so it continued to be the universal practice of the Church for many ages, upon the same symbolical reasons as it was first used by the apostles. St. Chrysostom proves the resurrection from this practice; 'for,' says he, 'our being baptized and immersed [$\varkappa\alpha\tau\alpha\delta\upsilon\varepsilon\sigma\theta\alpha\iota$] in the water, and our rising again out of it, is a symbol of our descending into hell, or the grave, and of our returning from thence.' Wherefore St. Paul calls baptism our burial. For says he, 'were buried with Christ by baptism into death.' And in another place, 'When we dip our heads in water as in a grave, our old man is buried; and when we rise up again, the new man rises therewith.' Cyril of Jerusalem makes it an emblem of the Holy Ghost's effusion upon the apostles: 'For as he that goes down into the water and is baptized and surrounded on all sides by the water, so the apostles were baptized all over by the Spirit: the water surrounds the body externally, but the Spirit incomprehensibly baptizes the interior soul.' It appears also from Epiphanius and others that almost all heretics who retained any baptism retained immersion also. The only heretics who did not observe a total immersion in baptism were the Eunomians, a branch of the Arians, of whom it was reported by Theodoret that they baptized only the upper parts of the body as far as the breast. And this they did in a very preposterous way, as Epiphanius relates, 'With their heels upward, and their head downward.' *So that these were the only men among all the heretics of the ancient Church that rejected this way of baptizing by a total immersion in ordinary cases.*[1] Indeed, the Church was so punctual to this rule that *we never read of any exception made to it in ordinary cases—no, not in the baptism of infants. For it appears in the 'Ordo Romanus' and Gregory's 'Sacramentarium' that infants as well as others were baptized by immersion; and the rules of the Church, except in cases of danger, do still require it.*

"But I must observe further that they not only administered baptism by immersion under water, but also repeated this three times. Tertullian speaks of it as a ceremony generally used in his time: 'We dip not once, but three times, at the naming of every person of the Trinity.' The same is asserted by St. Basil, St. Jerome, the author under the name of Dionysius; and St. Ambrose is most

---

[1] Yet this was an immersion as far as it went.—W. C.

particular in his description of trine immersion. Two reasons are commonly assigned for this practice: That it might represent Christ's three days' burial, and his resurrection on the third day, and that it might represent their profession of faith in the Holy Trinity, in whose name they were baptized.

"In the apostolic age, and some time after—before churches and baptisteries were generally erected—they baptized in any place where they had convenience. After this manner the author of the *Recognitions*, under the name of Clemens Romanus, represents Peter preaching to the people, and telling them that 'they might wash away their sins in the water of a river or a fountain or the sea when they were baptized, by invoking the name of the blessed Trinity upon them.'

"Baptisteries were anciently very capacious, because, as Dr. Cave truly observes, 'the stated times of baptism returning but seldom, there were usually great multitudes to be baptized at the same time.' And then the manner of baptizing by immersion, or dipping under water, made it necessary to have a large font likewise; whence the author of *The Chronicon Alexandrinum* styles the baptistery whither Basilicus fled the 'great illuminary;' which was indeed so capacious that we sometimes read of councils meeting and sitting therein."[1]

MILMAN AND IMMERSION.

This learned Episcopalian makes the following statements in regard to early baptismal usages:

"At Easter and at Pentecost, and in some places at the Epiphany, the rite of baptism was administered publicly to all the converts of the year, excepting those *few* instances in which it had been expedient to perform the ceremony without delay, or where the timid Christian put it off till the close of life. It was a complete lustration of the soul. The neophite *emerged from the waters of baptism* in a state of perfect innocence.

"The candidate approached the baptistery—in the larger churches a separate building. There he uttered the solemn vows which pledged him to his religion. The catechumen turned to the west, the realm of Satan [of darkness], and thrice renounced his power. He then turned to the east [the region of the rising sun], to adore the Sun of Righteousness and to proclaim his compact with the Lord of life. *The baptism was usually by immersion.*"[2]

[1] Bingham's *Antiquities of the Christian Church*, book viii. chap. 7, sec. 2; book xi. chap. 6, sec. 11; chap. 11, secs. 4–6.

[2] Milman's *History of Christianity*, p. 466. New York, 1841

Maitland's "Church in the Catacombs," and Immersion.

Maitland was an Episcopalian, whose sympathies were not drawn out toward the Baptists. He speaks of a stone "which seemed to have belonged *to a subterranean baptistery*," from which he quotes and translates the following inscription:

"The *living stream* cleanses the spots of the body, as well as of the heart, and at the same time washes away all [sin]."[1] Of course the stream that washed soul and body was the stream in which the baptismal immersion occurred. Elsewhere he says:

"*The immersion was required to be threefold, or trine*, as it was technically termed, and the renunciation of the devil and his works was thrice repeated."[2] This was the baptism of the ancient Roman Christians, according to Maitland.

In 1850 there was a Large Stone Baptistery in the Parish Church of Bradford, Yorkshire, England.

The vestibule of the sacred edifice was entered by an iron gate, and in it stood the baptistery, meeting

---

[1] *The Church in the Catacombs*, p. 221. London, 1846.
[2] *Ibid.*, p. 224.

the eye of every worshipper as he entered the building. The writer has seen this baptistery several times. It was a large block of stone *about* twelve feet long, *about* six feet wide, and *about* four feet high. On one side of it there was a cavity the necessary size for the immersion of an adult, and on the other an opening large enough for the immersion of a child of three years old. This block of stone, I was informed, was placed in the church by one of the vicars of Bradford about fifty years ago, to immerse a young lady of Baptist education who wished to unite with the Episcopal Church.

A friend, at my request, on a visit to Bradford, within a few months, went to the church to measure the stone, and there he learned that in repairing the church some time since the stone with two fonts had been broken up and removed.

IMMERSION IS THE ONLY AUTHORITATIVE AND LEGAL MODE OF BAPTISM FOR PERSONS OF SOUND HEALTH IN ENGLAND AT THIS HOUR.

The service prescribes that "The priest shall take the child into his hands, and shall say to the godfathers and godmothers, Name this child. And then, naming it after them (if they shall certify him that the child may well endure it), *he shall dip it in the water discreetly and warily;* but if they *certify that the child is weak,* it shall suffice to pour water upon it." [1]

Dipping is required by the ecclesiastical law of the Church of England, unless where the clergyman is certified that the child is weak. And as the Episcopal Church is established by act of Parliament as the church of the nation, its ceremonies have the force of civil laws; so that a healthy child which has never been baptized in any way, whose parents want it immersed, can *compel* by legal penalties the clergyman of their parish to immerse it.

---

[1] *Book of Common Prayer: Public Baptism of Infants.* Printed at the University Press, Oxford, 1863.

IRELAND.

Early Baptisms in Ireland.

The life of *St. Patrick, Apostle of Ireland*, by Dr. Todd, is a work of rare value. The author, at the time of publishing his book (1864), was senior fellow of Trinity College, Dublin, regius professor of Hebrew in that university, and, what is of far greater importance to us at present, a superior scholar in the Irish language and thoroughly acquainted with the scanty remains of ancient Irish literature. Of course he was an Episcopalian. He gives the following in regard to one of Patrick's baptisms:

"Patrick entered into the king's palace, and he said to Hercus [after some conversation], 'Wilt thou receive the baptism of the Lord, which I have with me?' He answered, 'I will receive it;' and *they came to the fountain Loigles,* and when he had opened his book and had *baptized the man Hercus,* he heard men behind his back mocking him one to another about the matter, for they knew not what he had done. And he baptized many thousand men on that day."[1] Now, why St. Patrick and

---

[1] *St. Patrick, Apostle of Ireland,* p. 442. Dublin, 1864.

Hercus should leave an Irish palace, even though it were but a hut, for baptismal purposes, and go to a fountain, is a puzzle, unless Hercus was immersed.

Todd mentions another baptism of St. Patrick: "Patrick then went to the place of assembly of the clan Amalgaidh, not far from the present town of Killala. Here, according to *The Tripartite Life*, he found a great assembly of the people with their chieftains. He stood up and addressed the multitude. He penetrated the hearts of all," says our author, "and led them to embrace cordially the Christian faith and doctrine. The seven sons of Amalgaidh, with the king himself and twelve thousand men, were baptized. *They were baptized in a well* [fountain] *called Tobur-en-adare.*"[1] Of course they were immersed, as they were *baptized in the well*. Nennius, in his *History of the Britons*, mentions "the baptism in one day of seven kings, the seven sons of Amalgaidh."[2] Nennius wrote at some period between the eighth and the tenth centuries.

ANOTHER BAPTISM BY ST. PATRICK.

Dr. Blackburn, in his *St. Patrick and the Early Irish Church*—a comparatively recent issue of the Presbyterian Board of Publication, Philadelphia—

[1] *St. Patrick, Apostle of Ireland*, p. 449. Dublin, 1864.
[2] Nennius's *History of the Britons*, p. 411. Bohn, London, 1848.

describes the kidnapping of some of St. Patrick's converts, just after their baptism, by Caroticus, or Carodoc, a Welsh man-stealer, as follows:

"It appears that one evening there was a multitude witnessing a baptism. A goodly number of converts *clad in white robes were at the fountain.* The minister, who seems not to have been Patrick, was baptizing them. Very soon after a band of pirates rushed upon them. Some were slain while the drops of water were scarcely dry *from their foreheads* [or from their clothing, for they were immersed]. Others were carried away in their white robes. The captives were taken to the seashore, put into boats, borne away into a foreign land, and sold into slavery."[1] Dr. Blackburn, by speaking of "drops of water on their foreheads," tries to leave the impression that these people were *sprinkled. But what brought them to the fountain, unless to enter it like Amalgaidh and his sons and all Christendom at the time?* The "Holy Wells" of Ireland were doubtless all ancient fonts of St. Patrick.

ANOTHER BAPTISM BY ST. PATRICK.

The Abbe McGeoghegan wrote a history of Ire-

[1] *St. Patrick and the Early Irish Church*, p. 188. Philadelphia.

land in French, which enjoys considerable credit and bears some merited censures. He gives an account of a baptism by St. Patrick near the future capital of Ireland. He says: "The high reputation of sanctity which St. Patrick had acquired, added to the number of miracles he wrought everywhere, having made him known and respected, even by the Pagans, the inhabitants of Dublin went out in crowds to him. These appearances were a happy omen of the faith they were about to receive from this saint. *He baptized them all*, with Alphin, son of Eochaid, who was at that time their king. *The ceremony was performed in a fountain near the city, called since that time the fountain of St. Patrick, and which became an object of devotion to the faithful for many centuries*, till it was filled up and enclosed within a private dwelling in the beginning of the seventeenth century. The saint had a church built near this fountain, which afterward became a cathedral, bearing his name."[1]

St. Patrick's Cathedral in Dublin, built about A. D. 1190, is still standing. St. Patrick in A. D. 448 immersed a throng in this fountain. On examination of Archbishop Usher's work, to which the Abbe McGeoghegan refers as an authority, we find that the learned primate of Ireland " saw himself the fountain

[1] McGeoghegan's *History of Ireland*, p. 145. Dublin, 1849.

of St. Patrick, which had very lately in his time been enclosed and filled up within a private house."[1] The archbishop also speaks on the same page of the baptism of the seven sons of Amalgaidh. And just as the neighborhood of the Lady's Well in Northumberland, England, where Paulinus immersed three thousand persons at the Easter of A. D. 627, was selected as the site of a Benedictine nunnery, so a church was erected near this holy fountain to commemorate the grand event, and to gather the blessings which were supposed to come from such a blessed consecration.

Immersions Recorded by Father O'Farrell.

The Reverend Michael J. O'Farrell, in his *Popular Life of St. Patrick*, dedicated to Monsignor Woodlock, rector of the Irish Catholic University in Dublin, and published in 1863 by D. & J. Sadlier of New York, speaking of the Irishman who had just renounced Paganism for Christianity, says: "At every step, indeed, the transition to the new faith was smoothed by such coincidences or adoptions. The convert saw *in the baptismal font when he was immersed the sacred well* at which his fathers had wor-

---

[1] Illum Patricii fontem vidimus (intra privatas ædes inclusum nuperime et obstructum), *Britannic. Eccles. Antiquit.*, p. 449. London, 1687.

shipped."[1] St. Patrick's font, according to Father O'Farrell, was a well, and his baptism immersion.

Speaking of a celebrated Irish idol called Cean Croithi—that is, the head of all the gods—made of gold and silver, around which twelve inferior gods of brass stood, which St. Patrick destroyed at a time when great numbers of persons were present, O'Farrell says: "And many, beholding it, believed in the true and living God, and being baptized, according to the apostle, 'put on Christ.' And in that place St. Patrick by his prayers produced out of the earth a *fountain of the clearest water, wherein many were afterward baptized.*"[2]

St. Patrick ascended the mountain Croagh Patrick, in county Mayo, for prayer and religious meditation, and, according to O'Farrell, " after descending from the mountain, invigorated for the sacred duties of the ministry, St. Patrick came to the district of Corcothemne—not far distant, it would seem —and *to the fountain of Sinn, where he baptized many thousands.*"[3]

O'Farrell gives the following account of the conversion and baptism of the Amalgaidhs and many others, already mentioned : " When the saint entered Tirawly, the seven sons [of Amalgaidh] assembled

---

[1] *Popular Life of St. Patrick*, p. 110. New York, 1863.
[2] *Ibid.*, p. 135.   [3] *Ibid.*, p. 157.

with their followers. Profiting by the presence of so vast a multitude, the apostle entered into the midst of them, his soul inflamed with the love of God, and with a celestial courage preached unto them the truths of Christianity; and so powerful was the effect of his burning words that the seven princes and over twelve thousand men were converted on that day, and *were soon after baptized in a well called Tobar-Enadhaire, the well of Enadhaire.*"[1]

At another time, when St. Patrick was near Lough Neagh, he was opposed by a chieftain named Carthen, and compelled to leave the neighborhood; but his younger brother listened to the divine word and became a convert. "Of him, perhaps," says O'Farrell, "the following is related: While on a certain time the saint was *baptizing in the holy font a chief named Curtan, together with his wife,* he foretold to the woman that she should have a daughter to whom he would give the veil."[2]

Preaching in Ulster, a robber band, seeing him on a journey, first thought of stealing everything he might possess, but moved with compassion, they changed their minds, and pretended that one of their company who feigned to be dead was really gone into the world of spirits; and for amusement they

[1] *Popular Life of St. Patrick,* p. 163. New York, 1863.
[2] *Ibid.,* p. 182.

plead with Patrick to restore him to life. The Irish apostle understood the trick, and earnestly prayed for the man's conversion; and as Patrick went his way, as O'Farrell says, "the wretched man, Garbanus, was no more. His pretence was turned into a reality, and they saw before them the corpse of their luckless companion. Affrighted lest the same should happen to them, they followed the saint and fell at his feet, and by their contrition obtained pardon. They all believed in the Lord, and in his name they were baptized. Then did the saint revive the dead man, *and baptizing him in the holy font*, associated him unto them in the faith of Christ." [1]

We do not assert the truth of all these incidents in the life of St. Patrick, though some of them are undoubted facts; but his baptism, when described to any extent, *is in a fountain, in a well, or it is plainly declared to be immersion.* St. Patrick gives an account of his own conversion in his *Confession*, just as a regenerated candidate for baptism in a Baptist church would. He required apparently the same regeneration in his converts, and then he immersed them. The story of his life makes him so like a Baptist missionary that we believe he was one.

[1] *Popular Life of St. Patrick*, pp. 238, 239. N. Y., 1863.

The Irish Immersed Three Times in Water or in Milk.

Michelet needs no commendation as a historian of great learning and of unusual exactness. He says of the ancient Irish that their "*infants were thrice plunged in water, or in milk if the parents were wealthy.*" [1]

Gilbert, Bishop of Limerick in Ireland, on Immersion.

Gilbert was a correspondent of Anselm, the godly and learned Archbishop of Canterbury. He lived in the early part of the twelfth century. In his little work on *The Constitution of the Church* he writes of the priest:

"It is his duty to administer baptism, *to dip* believers who have been exorcised and who have confessed the Holy Trinity, *with three immersions in the sacred font.*" [2]

---

[1] Michelet's *History of France*, vol. ii. p. 102. New York, 1869.

[2] Sub trina immersione sacro fonte intingere. *St. Anselmus, Patrol. Lat.*, vol. 159, p. 1000. Migne. Parisiis.

AMERICA.

JOHN WESLEY AND IMMERSION.

A COUPLE of curious facts are recorded by Mr. Wesley, in his journal, in connection with the baptism of two children. While he was in Georgia, in 1736, he makes this record:

"Saturday, 21st February.—Mary Welsh, aged eleven days, was baptized, *according to the custom of the first church and the rule of the Church of England, by immersion.* The child was ill then, but recovered from that hour."[1] In the following May he writes:

"Wednesday, May 5th.—I was asked to baptize a child of Mr. Parker, second bailiff of Savannah. But Mrs. Parker told me, 'Neither Mr. Parker nor I will consent to its being dipped.' I answered, 'If you certify that your child is weak, it will suffice, the Rubric says, to pour water upon it.' She replied, 'Nay, the child is not weak, but I am resolved it shall not be dipped.' This argument I could not confute. *So I went home,* and the child

[1] *Wesley's Works,* vol. i. p. 130. Philadelphia, 1826.

was baptized *by another person.*"[1] Mr. Wesley immerses Mary Welsh "according to the custom of the first church and the rule of the Church of England," and he requires an assurance from the mother of another child, which he is requested to baptize, that it is weak, before he can set aside the rule of the English Church which demanded immersion; and on the mother's declaration that the child is not weak, he goes away without baptizing it, another performs the office, and Mr. Wesley clearly leaves us to understand that in his opinion immersion was an imperative mode of baptism in every case where there was not satisfactory evidence of weakness.

A Baptism in Brooklyn, New York.

A Baptist lady of superior intelligence gives the following very interesting account of an immersion by the Rev. Henry Ward Beecher in his own church in Brooklyn:

"Being in Brooklyn for a few days, I have had the opportunity of witnessing a baptism by immersion, the administrator being none other than the Rev. Henry Ward Beecher. Twenty-five years ago, shortly after he became pastor of Plymouth Church, he avowed his willingness to administer the rite of

[1] *Wesley's Works*, vol. i. p. 134. Philadelphia, 1826.

baptism by immersion to any one who preferred it. For some years, by the courtesy of the pastors, Mr. Beecher used the baptisteries of Baptist churches. But at a time when the edifice of Plymouth Church was undergoing repairs he expressed a desire that a baptistery should be placed in it, that they might not be dependent on the kindness of their friends. His request was cheerfully acceded to. On his large pulpit platform stands a movable desk, table, and chair. On setting these aside and turning up the carpet, a long door is seen, the opening of which uncovers the pool, with steps at each end for descending and ascending. On the occasion when I was present—and I was told that it was the usual custom—the ordinance was administered after the Friday evening prayer-meeting. At the close of the service on that evening Mr. Beecher mentioned in the simplest manner that candidates were to be baptized, and he invited the congregation to repair to the main audience-room. This large room, holding three thousand persons, of course was not filled, but there were perhaps five hundred persons there. The room was lighted principally at the point where the interest centred. There was a solemn stillness while the people waited for the coming of the administrator. The candidates were but two, a young man and a young woman. Their youthful appearance and peaceful countenances added to the interest of the scene. After singing and prayer he led them down successively into the water and immersed them in the name of the Trinity.

"His views on the subject are well known. He believes that baptism is typical, and that the application of water in any form answers the requirement. But never were candidates more completely *buried* in baptism than those I saw laid in the liquid grave by Mr. Beecher; and none who heard his solemn tones and noticed the interest he took in his part of the ceremony could doubt that he felt he was fulfilling the Saviour's command—'Teach all nations, baptizing them.' His manner was characterized by simplicity and reverence, and there was nothing to distinguish it from the same ordinance as administered by any regular Baptist minister. Although I have witnessed many baptisms in the course of my life, this, from the outward circumstances, was of peculiar interest to me, and one not soon to be forgotten."

COLEMAN ON IMMERSION.

The Rev. Lyman Coleman, D. D., for many years a professor in Lafayette College, Pennsylvania, is the author of a work of considerable merit on Christian antiquities. Dr. Coleman is a Presbyterian minister, "past eighty years of age at the present time, highly esteemed in the community in which he resides, and revered by his Presbyterian brethren. He is a man of deliberation and candor, and his opinions have much weight among his people."[1]

Writing of immersion, Professor Coleman says:

"We cannot resist the conviction that this mode of baptism was the first *departure* from the teaching and example of the apostles on this subject. . . . *If it was a departure from their teachings,* it was the earliest, *for baptism by immersion unquestionably was very early the common mode of baptism.*"

"*Trine immersion.*—*In the second century* it had become *customary to immerse three times*, at the mention of the several names in the Godhead. This is only an expansion of the idea of the indispensable importance of immersion, and indicates more fully the foreign origin of this rite."[2]

"In the primitive church, *immediately subsequent to the age of the apostles*, immersion, or dipping, was undeniably the *common mode of baptism.* The *utmost* that can be said of *sprinkling* in that early period is, *that it was in case of necessity permitted*

---

[1] From a Baptist friend of Dr. Coleman.
[2] *Ancient Christianity Exemplified*, pp. 366, 368. Philadelphia, 1852.

as an exception to a general rule. This fact is so well established that it were needless to adduce authorities in proof of it.

"It is a *great mistake* to suppose that baptism by *immersion was discontinued* when infant baptism became generally prevalent. The practice of *immersion continued even until the thirteenth or fourteenth century.* Indeed, it has never been formally abandoned, but *is still the mode of administering infant baptism in the Greek Church and in several of the Eastern churches.*

"After the lapse of several centuries, aspersion, or sprinkling, gradually took the place of immersion without any established rule of the Church or formal renunciation of the rite of immersion. The form was not esteemed essential to the validity of the ordinance. The Eastern Church, however, in direct opposition to these views, has uniformly retained the form of immersion as indispensable to the validity of the ordinance, and repeated the rite whenever they have received to their communion persons who had been previously baptized in another manner."[1]

Professor Coleman in these declarations speaks as an honest man who had read the writings of the

[1] *Ancient Christianity Exemplified*, pp. 395–397. Philadelphia, 1852.

first twelve hundred years of the Christian era, which were penned by the followers of the Saviour. He who speaks otherwise has not surveyed the rich and large harvest-field of testimony, or he misrepresents it. It is due to Professor Coleman to state that he contends as ably as any man could with such miserable witnesses that immersion was not Christ's mode of baptism or that of his apostles. "Immersion was the first *departure* from the teaching and example of the apostles." . . . "If it was a departure." "Immediately *subsequent to the age of the apostles* immersion, or dipping, was undeniably the common mode of baptism." But he nowhere admits that it was the mode of administering baptism approved by the apostles.

Dr. Coleman declares that "aspersion [sprinkling] did not become general in the West until the thirteenth century, though it appears to have been introduced some time before that period. Thomas Aquinas [he died A. D. 1274] says: 'It is safer to baptize by immersion, because this is the general practice. Tutius est baptizare per modum immersionis, quia hoc habet communis usus.'"[1] The celebrated St. Thomas, whom Dr. Coleman quotes, does not agree with the professor of Lafayette, that

[1] Coleman's *Ancient Christianity Exemplified*, p. 398. Philadelphia, 1852.

aspersion was "*general* in the thirteenth century." He expressly declares, in his own clear words and in Dr. Coleman's translation, that *immersion is the general practice.* We have, however, the testimony of Professor Coleman that immersion was the general mode of baptism throughout the whole Christian Church down to the end of the twelfth century, and *that* from the time "immediately subsequent to the age of the apostles, immersion, or dipping, was undeniably the common mode of baptism."

FRANCE.

The Conversion and Baptism of Clovis.

BEFORE the conversion of Clovis he was the chieftain of a small tribe of the Franks of Tournai. In a time of great danger the different tribes united together under a chieftain of their choice and made war upon the common foe. But the union ended with the close of the war, if it held together so long. The kingdom of France had no existence before the conversion of Clovis, and the royal rulers of sections of the Franks were often treated with as little ceremony as the lowliest members of their clans.[1] Clovis was a brave and ambitious warrior, determined to extend his authority and his territory. The aim of his life was to subdue all his neighbors and become the head of a great empire.

In A. D. 496, the Alemanni threatened to cross the Rhine; the Franks gathered from all quarters to resist them. Clovis was elected general of their army. They attacked the Alemanni[2] at Zülpich,

[1] Michelet's *History of France*, vol. i. pp. 84, 85. New York, 1869.

[2] Neander's *History of the Christian Religion and Church*, iii. 8. Boston, 1869.

about twenty-two miles south-west of Cologne, and for a time the situation of the Franks was desperate. Clovis vainly appealed to the gods for assistance. As a last resort he cried to Christ, the God of his truly pious wife Clotilda, and soon the army of the Alemanni was killed or captured, and Clovis gathered increased military glory from his victory in this deadly conflict.

He appears with all honesty to have believed that Christ gave him his triumph in the battle of Zülpich, and soon after he was baptized—a rough, bloody, and most probably unconverted man, but a sincere believer in the might and rule of Jesus over the nations. From that battle it was everywhere spread abroad that Christ was on the side of Clovis. The Christian clergy were active in giving currency to these representations. The king was grateful to Christ and a munificent benefactor of his churches for his divine assistance; and Clovis, aided by the prestige of victory, by confidence in his new God, and by the active efforts of all the Christian communities scattered throughout France, marched in triumph over the territories of his enemies, sweeping away hostile armies and Pagan gods and priests, and rearing a magnificent French and Christian empire—Christian only in part; but the part of Christianity planted in the days of

Clovis finally produced most of the other fair portions of the system of Jesus. Avitus of Vienne, Gregory of Tours, Alcuin, and Hincmar of Rheims will furnish us with some facts about the baptism of Clovis.

Avitus of Vienne and the Immersion of Clovis.

Bishop Avitus occupied the see of Vienne in the end of the fifth century and in the beginning of the sixth. He was useful in reclaiming leading Arians from their heresy and in advancing the general welfare of the Frankish Church. He wrote a letter to Clovis congratulating him on his baptism, in which he says:

"That it might appear in due order that you were *born again out of the water* for salvation on that day [Christmas Day] on which the world received the Lord of heaven, born for its redemption."[1]

In the baptism of Clovis, of which Avitus writes, the king was born again *out of the water*—that is, he was immersed in it and *lifted up out of it*.

---

[1] Regenerari ex unda. *Ep. Aviti Viennen., Episc., ad Clod. Regem. S. Greg., Touronensis opera omnia*, Appendix. *Patrol. Lat.*, vol. 71, p. 1154.

Gregory of Tours and the Immersion of Clovis.

Gregory was descended from an illustrious family, and became Bishop of Tours in A.D. 574. His uncle, Gallus, was Bishop of Clermont. Gregory wrote a history of the Franks in ten books, which has been repeatedly published, and which was reissued ten years since in the *Patrologiæ Latinæ*, the finest collection of Christian Latin writers ever given to the world. "*The History of Gregory*," says Dupin, "is very useful, and contains many things of great consequence."[1] In this work he gives the following account of the baptism of Clovis:

"The queen did not cease to charge the king that he should know the true God, and that he should despise idols; but he could by no means be moved to believe these things until at last war was stirred up against the Alemanni, in which he was compelled by necessity to confess that which, of his free will, he had previously denied. Moreover, it came to pass that when both armies were hotly engaged there was a great slaughter, and the army of Clovis began to rush to sure destruction; but he, seeing this, pained at the heart, moved to tears, and with eyes lifted up to the heavens, said: 'O Jesus Christ, whom Clotilda

---

[1] Dupin's *Ecclesiastical History*, i. 561. Dublin, 1723.

declares to be the Son of the living God, thou who art said to give help to the struggling and victory to those hoping in thee; devoted to thee, I entreat the glory of thy assistance; and if thou wilt indulge me with victory over these enemies, and I shall have full experience of that valor which the people dedicated to thy name proclaim that they have put to the proof, I shall believe upon thee, and I shall be baptized in thy name. For I have called upon my gods, and they have been far from helping me; from which consideration I believe that the gods who do not come to those obeying them are invested with no power. Now I call upon thee, and I desire to believe upon thee, only let me not be overthrown by my adversaries.' And when he said these things, the Alemanni began to seek flight; and when they perceived that their king was killed, they put themselves under the authority of Clovis, saying, 'We entreat that no more people may be killed; we are thine.' But he, when the war was prohibited and the people collected together, returning with peace, informed the queen in what way he was enabled to secure the victory, by the invocation of Christ's name. Then the queen secretly ordered St. Remigius, Bishop of Rheims, to be brought, entreating him to recommend the word of salvation to the king.

"The priest, when brought, began secretly to ad

vise him to believe on the true God, the Creator of heaven and earth, to despise idols, which were of no service either to him or to others. But he said, 'Most holy father, I can hear you joyfully. There is, however, one difficulty; the people who follow me will not permit me to forsake their gods. But I will go and speak to them about your proposal.' Meeting with his people, the power of God ran before him before he uttered a word. The whole people shouted together, 'We cast away mortal gods, O pious king, and we are prepared to follow the immortal God whom Remigius proclaims!' These things were communicated to the chief priest, who, full of great joy, ordered the [baptismal] *laver*[1] to be prepared. The wide streets to the church were shaded by painted canvas and adorned with white curtains, the baptistery was put in order, balsam was poured out, burning wax-lights with a sweet odor shone, and the whole *temple of the baptistery*[2] was sprinkled with a celestial perfume, and God bestowed such favor upon those standing there that they reckoned that they were placed beside the odors of paradise. Then the king demanded that he should be baptized first by the pontiff. The new Constantine proceeded to the *laver*, about to blot out the disease of ancient leprosy and the filthy stains borne a long time, in *a*

[1] Lavacrum.   [2] Templum baptisterii.

fresh fountain.[1] The saint of God addressed him as he walked to baptism with eloquent lips, saying, 'O Sicamber, meekly bow thy head; adore what thou hast burned, burn what thou hast adored.' For the holy Bishop Remigius was a man of eminent knowledge, and especially imbued with rhetorical tastes; but he was also so distinguished for sanctity that he was regarded in virtues as the equal of holy Silvester. For there is now the book of his life which tells that he was awakened from the dead. Therefore the king, confessing the omnipotent God in the Trinity, was baptized in the name of the Father, and of the Son, and of the Holy Spirit."

"From his army there were baptized more than three thousand; and his sister Albofledis was baptized."[2]

The "*laver*" in which Clovis was baptized is literally *a bath,* and could not be used to represent a basin for sprinkling or pouring. But Gregory describes his own view of the mode of baptism very clearly in the following curious miracle which occurred somewhere in Spain, if it is not a fable: " The bishop and the citizens found the [baptismal]

[1] Recenti latice. *S. Gregor. Episc. Turonem., Hist. Franc.,* lib. secund. cap. 31; *Patrol. Lat.,* v. 71, pp. 226, 227. Migne. Parisiis.

[2] *Ibid.,* lib. ii. cap. 30, 31 ; *Patrol. Lat.,* vol. 71, pp. 225-227.

pool full which they had left empty, and the [water] rising in a heap higher than its sides, as when a measure of wheat is heaped up above its mouth; and you could see the waters rippling hither and thither, and not flowing in an opposite direction.

"All the people out of devotion drink, and carry home a vessel full for their health; and they protect their fields and vines by a very wholesome sprinkling; and after an uncounted multitude of *amphoræ* were filled, not yet even is the heap [of waters] diminished. Howbeit, when the first infant was immersed the water began to withdraw."[1]

The word which Gregory uses for pool is *piscina*, a *fishpond*, from *piscis*, a fish. The same word is often used to describe a pool, a cistern, a tank; and in this *piscina the infant is immersed*. That was Gregory's mode of baptism for Clovis and all other recipients of that sacrament.

Alcuin's Account of the Immersion of Clovis.

In his *Life of St. Vedastus*, Alcuin informs us that Clovis received religious instruction from that saint, and that he recommended him to St. Remigius for

[1] Piscina . . . infans primus intinctus fuerit. *S. Greg. Turonen. Episc. Mirac.*, lib. i. cap. 24; *De Gloria Mart., Patrol. Lat.*, vol. 71, p. 725. Migne. Parisiis.

further enlightenment. Writing of the baptism of the king of the Franks, Alcuin says:

"The king, with no doubts about the faith, with great alacrity, with eagerness on the way, hastened to see the most holy pontiff Remigius, that by his most sacred ministry, through the power of the divine Spirit, he might be washed in the living fountain of catholic baptism for the remission of sins and for the hope of eternal life. He led the eager king to the fountain of life, and when he came *he washed him in the fountain* of eternal salvation [baptism]. So the king was baptized with his nobles and people, who rejoiced to receive the sacrament of *the healing bath,* divine grace having been previously given them."[1] The man who is washed *in a fountain or in a font* is clearly not sprinkled with water, nor does he receive the pouring of water for baptism in such a situation.

In a letter to the canons of Lyons, Alcuin represents a man as becoming one of the catechumens when formerly he had been a Pagan, and then in the name of the Trinity "*he is baptized by trine immersion.*"[2] And when he represents Clovis as

[1] In fonte salutis eternæ venientem abluebat. Alcuinus, *Vita St. Vedast., Patrol. Lat.,* vol. 101, pp. 686–690. Migne. Parisiis.

[2] Trina submersione baptizatur. *Alcuini Epistolæ,* ep. 90; *Patrol. Lat.,* vol. 100, pp. 289, 290.

washed in a fountain, he means that "he was *baptized by trine immersion* in a fountain"—the only baptism which Alcuin was accustomed to tolerate.

THE IMMERSION OF CLOVIS, AS DESCRIBED BY HINCMAR OF RHEIMS, WHOSE PREDECESSOR, ST. REMIGIUS, BAPTIZED THE KING.

The baptism of Clovis took place at Rheims, and it is probable that it equalled in grandeur any baptismal service in Christian history, and that it surpassed every other similar scene except two or three.

Hincmar, Archbishop of Rheims in the first half of the ninth century, living in the place where the memorable baptism occurred, and the successor of the bishop who officiated at it—a writer with every qualification to give a correct account of the most prominent and influential event in French history —describes the baptism of Clovis as follows:

"In the mean time the way leading to the baptistery was put in order. On both sides it was hung with painted canvas and curtains; overhead there was a protecting shade; the streets were levelled; the baptistery of the church was prepared for the occasion, and sprinkled with balsam and other perfumes.

"Moreover, the Lord bestowed favor on the people, that they might think that they were refreshed with the sweet odors of paradise.

"And the holy pontiff Remigius, holding the hand of the king, went forth from the royal residence to the baptistery, followed by the queen and the people, the holy Gospels going before them, with all hymns and spiritual songs and litanies, and with the names of the saints loudly invoked. Moreover, whilst they proceeded together the king interrogated the bishop, saying, 'Patron, is this the kingdom of God which you promised me?' And the bishop said, 'This is not that kingdom, but the beginning of the way by which you approach it.' The new Constantine advanced to the healing font in which the leprosy of chronic disease and the filth of the ancient pollution of iniquity might be completely removed. The blessed Remigius officiated on the solemn occasion, by whom, in apostolic doctrine and in a holy life, another Silvester[1] seemed to be represented.

"Clovis having entered the life-giving fountain, the holy bishop delivered this eloquent address: 'O Sicamber, meekly bow thy head, and adore what thou hast burned, and burn what thou hast adored.' Framing salutary laws, with lowly reverence he

[1] In allusion to a fable, believed for centuries in Western Europe, that Pope Silvester baptized Constantine the Great.

honored the churches built for religious worship, that he might adore God in the houses which with fierce profanity he was accustomed to give to the flames. . . . After confessing the orthodox faith in answer to questions put by the holy pontiff, *according to ecclesiastical custom he was baptized by trine immersion*,[1] in the name of the holy and undivided Trinity—Father, Son, and Holy Spirit; and, received by the pontiff himself from the holy font, he was anointed with sacred chrism, with the sign of the holy cross of our Lord Jesus Christ.

"Moreover, from his army three thousand men were baptized, without counting women and children. His sisters also, Albofledis and Landeheldis, were baptized; and there was great rejoicing that day among holy angels in heaven and godly men on earth.

"Finally, a great host of the Franks, not yet converted to the faith, lived with Regnarius for some time beyond the river Somme. King Clovis, having gained famous victories, killed Regnarius, who was covered with flagitious crimes, and who had been delivered to him bound by the Franks; and he induced all the Frankish people, through the

---

[1] Secundum ecclesiasticam morem baptizatus est trina mersione. *Vita Sanct. Remig., Patrol. Lat.*, vol. 125, pp. 1160-1161. Migne. Parisiis.

blessed Remigius, to be converted to the faith and to be baptized."

The Rev. George W. Anderson, D. D., of this city, at my request gives the following account of the baptistery in Paris, represented by tradition to be the one in which Clovis was baptized:

"The baptistery in which Clovis is said to have submitted to the ordinance has long been in the Bibliothèque Nationale in Paris. My attention was called to it some years ago, but I never saw it till the summer of 1872. On that occasion I visited the library and made a careful examination of the bath. It is of polished porphyry, fully seven feet long, about two and a half feet deep, and nearly the same in width. There can be no doubt of its suitableness for the purpose. In the latter part of March in the same year I had seen three men baptized in Rome by the Rev. James Wall, the English Baptist missionary in that city. The baptistery was smaller in every way than the one in Paris, but it was quite large enough for the due observance of the ordinance. As to the authority on which it is said to have been used on the occasion of the baptism of Clovis, I cannot give any information."

This vessel was *probably* used for the baptism of Clovis, his sisters, his warriors, and a number of women and children; and that *immersion was the mode of baptism* by which the king and so many of his people were initiated into the Christian Church *is beyond all doubt*, whether this laver was used or not.

ARCHBISHOP MAGNUS OF SENS, AND IMMERSION.

Magnus was honored by being consecrated by the pope himself, Leo III., at Rome, A. D. 801. By order of Charlemagne he prepared a work on baptism for the information of the clergy and the faithful. In this treatise he says:

"*Baptism in Greek is translated immersion in Latin,* . . . and therefore *the infant is immersed three times in the sacred font, that trine immersion* may mystically show forth the three days' burial of Christ, and that the lifting up from the waters may be a likeness of Christ rising from the tomb."[1]

The account given by Magnus of baptism, which is quoted above, has the same ideas and chiefly the same words as were given to Charlemagne by one of his bishops, and appear in this work. But there are verbal variations in the original Latin which indicate two authors.

[1] Baptismum Græce Latine tinctio interpretatur . . . infans ter mergitur in sacro fonte ut sepulturam triduanam Christi trina demersio mystice designaret, et ab aquis elevatio Christi resurgentis similitudo est de sepulcro. *Patrol. Lat.*, vol. 102, p. 981. Migne. Parisiis.

Leidradus, Bishop of Lyons, on Baptism, A. D. 816.

This author has left us three epistles and a tract on baptism. He was a man of distinction among the ecclesiastics of his day. He was sent twice into Spain by Charlemagne to reclaim Felix and Elipandus, who taught that Christ as a man was the Son of God only in name and by adoption. Speaking of baptism, he says:

"But we *immerse three times* that we may show forth the mystery of the three days' burial; that whilst the infant is drawn out of the water three times, the resurrection [at the close] of three days may be shown forth, . . . in the baptism of infants there ought to be no censure for *immersing once or thrice, since in three immersions* the Trinity of persons [in the Godhead] can be exhibited, and in a single immersion the oneness of Jehovah."[1]

Theodulphus, Bishop of Orleans, on Immersion.

Theodulphus, an Italian who enjoyed the special friendship of Charlemagne and of Louis the Pious,

[1] Nos autem tertio mergimus . . . infantum in baptismate vel ter vel semel mergere; quando in tribus mersionibus personarum trinitas, et in una potest divinitatis singularitas designari. *Leidrad. Episc. Lugdun., Patrol. Lat.*, vol. 99, p. 863. Migne. Parisiis.

became Bishop of Orleans A. D. 794, and died A. D. 821. He wrote several works in prose and poetry. There is still in existence a beautiful copy of the Holy Scriptures which was prepared at his expense, and to which he prefixed a preface and some poems in golden letters. In his tract *On Baptism* he says:

"We are buried with Christ when, at the invocation of the Holy Trinity, *we descend by trine immersion into the font of the laver as if into a certain grave.* When divested [by baptism] of all sins *as we go out from the font, we arise with Christ.*"[1]

HINCMAR AND IMMERSION.

Two French bishops in the ninth century bore this name. Hincmar, Bishop of Laon, was arrogant and quarrelsome. He had bitter controversies with the king, his clergy, and his uncle until he was deposed. Hincmar, Archbishop of Rheims, the uncle of Hincmar of Laon, was a man of superior intellect and culture, and of very great influence in the Church and in the State. He gives his views of baptism in the following words:

"*If you believe and confess three immersions* in the

[1] Sub trina immersione in fonte lavacri, quasi in quoddam sepulcrum descendimus . . . de fonte quasi egredimur. *Theodulf. Aurelian. Episc., Patrol. Lat.*, vol. 105, p. 223. Migne. Parisiis.

name of the Holy Trinity, Father, Son, and Sacred Spirit, *to be one baptism*, because there is one God. the Father and Son and Holy Spirit, of one essence, of one Deity, of one nature, in whose name catholic baptism is administered—. . . . if you are silent about this question, *we shall therefore say that the three immersions are one baptism.*"[1] Hincmar is defending the Trinity.

Baptism of Hastein, a Danish Pirate, in France, a. d. 887.

In the *Flowers of History*, written by Roger of Wendover, a monk of St. Alban's, in the thirteenth century, we have an account of the ravages and murders perpetrated by Hastein, or Hasting, in England and France; and to crown all his infamies Roger records his impious baptism. He says:

"At length he sent his servants to the Bishop and Count of Lunis [a French city he vainly tried to capture], informing them that he was seized with a mortal illness, and humbly requesting to be made a Christian by them. On hearing this, the bishop and count rejoiced greatly, and making peace with the enemy of peace, allowed his people free admis-

---

[1] Tres mersiones. . . . Dicimus ideo tres mersiones unum esse baptisma. *Hincm. Rhem., De Una et Non Trina Dictate., Patrol. Lat.*, vol. 125, pp. 554, 555. Migne. Parisiis.

sion to the city. At length the wicked Hastein was carried to the church *and immersed in the sacred font, from which the bishop and mayor raised him again* to their own destruction; and after receiving the holy anointing he was carried back to his ships by the hands of his servants. After this, in the depth of night he was clad in armor and laid on a bier, having directed his followers to wear their coats of mail under their tunics. His comrades then with feigned sorrow bore him from on board ship to the church, where the bishop in his holy garments was ready to sacrifice the host for the deceased; when, behold, Hastein, that son of perdition, suddenly sprang up from the bier, put the bishop and count to the sword, and fell with wolfish rage on the people."[1]

The Immersion of a Pirate.

Richerus, a monk of Rheims, in the tenth century, the author of a history in four books, gives the following description of the baptism of one of the numerous outlaws who at that time infested the coasts and rivers of Europe:

"On the appointed day, in the basilica of St. Marcial the Martyr, the services of the bishops

[1] *Roger of Wendover*, at A. D. 887, vol. i., pp. 223, 224. London, 1849.

being over, he [a pirate], received from the king himself, *descended into the holy font, and was baptized by trine immersion* in the name of the Father and of the Son and of the Holy Spirit."[1]

St. Fulbert and Immersion.

St. Fulbert, Bishop of Chartres, in the beginning of the eleventh century, was a warm friend to learning and theology. He gave lectures to the public on various important subjects in the schools of the church of Chartres. Throngs of students from France and Germany went forth from his instructions to extend his fame and enlighten the benighted.

Robert, King of France, highly esteemed St. Fulbert, and for nearly a quarter of a century he was the honored head of the church of Chartres. Expounding Romans vi. 3, 4—" Know ye not that so many of us as were baptized into Christ, were baptized into his death? Therefore we are buried with him by baptism into death, that like as Christ was raised from the dead by the glory of the Father, even so we also should walk in newness of life," etc.—he says:

"As, therefore, we have been informed that the

[1] In sacrum fontem descenderet . . . trina immersione. *Hist.*, lib. iv.; *Patrol. Lat.*, vol. 138, p. 24. Migne. Parisiis.

body of our Lord Jesus Christ was buried in an earthly grave three days and three nights, *so also a man immersed three times under an element allied to the earth [water] is covered; and thus, whilst he is immersed in imitation of a vital mystery, he is buried; when he is raised [from the water] he is awakened.* In connection with this topic, reflect a little upon what the water accomplishes and upon what the Holy Spirit performs: *The water brings down the person dying, as it were, into the tomb; the Holy Spirit brings him, as if rising again, through to heaven.*"[1] At this period, from end to end of Christendom, baptism was thus described.

Ivo, Bishop of Chartres, and Immersion.

Ivo was a man of extensive learning and of unusual reverence for the old customs of the Church. His morals were unblemished, and his influence was great in every department of his country and among all classes of society. He died A. D. 1115.

Writing of baptism, he quotes the language of Pope Leo the Great as his own:

[1] Et homo ita sub cognato terræ elemento trina vice demersus operitur, ac sic vitalis imitatione mysterii dum demergitur sepelitur. . . . Aqua velut morientem deducit in tumulum; Spiritus Sanctus velut resurgentum perducit ad coelum. *S. Fulberti Carnot. Episc. Ep.; Patrol. Lat.*, vol. 141, p. 200. Migne. Parisiis.

"*Trine immersion is an imitation of the three days' burial, and the rising from the waters is a likeness of the resurrection from the sepulchre.*"[1]

Gregory the Great and Leo the Great are quoted very frequently before and during the twelfth century as authorities on the baptismal question.

HUGO OF ST. VICTOR AND IMMERSION.

Hugo was born A. D. 1096, and died A. D. 1140. He was a monk of the monastery of St. Victor in Paris, and one of the most prominent literary men in Europe in the twelfth century. His works are numerous, and treat of theology, philosophy, and other questions. He was a great admirer of St. Augustine; and such was his reputation that obscure authors placed his name upon their productions to secure for them the respect paid to the works of such a distinguished writer. Treating of baptism, he states that "*trine immersion* itself is spoken of as the sacrament of the Trinity or of the three days' burial [of Christ]. *Immersion is made baptism by the invocation of the Trinity.* After you promised to believe *we immersed your heads three times in the sacred font*"[2] [candidates for baptism were

---

[1] Sepulturam triduanam imitatur trina demersio. *De Fide, Patrol. Lat.*, vol. 161, p. 73. Migne. Parisiis.

[2] Ipsa trina immersio sacramentum dicitur vel Trinitatis

placed in the water up to the neck by deacons if men, or by deaconesses if women, after which the bishop came and dipped their heads in the water]. "This order of baptism is observed to show forth a double mystery; *for ye were rightly immersed three times* who have received baptism in the name of the Trinity, *and ye were rightly immersed three times* who have received baptism in the name of Jesus Christ, who arose from the dead on the third day; *for this trine immersion is a figure of the Lord's burial*, through which [immersion] ye have been buried with Christ by baptism."[1]

Hugo then proceeds to quote the letter of Gregory the Great to Leander, approving of one immersion in Spanish baptisms, though he admits that in Rome they had three. He also cites Haymo, Bishop of Halberstadt, who declares in his *Commentary on the Epistle to the Romans* that "he immersed little children once in baptism."

In another place Hugo, addressing the adminis-

vel . . . baptismus immersio facta est. . . . Postquam vos credere promisistis tertio capita vestra in sacro fonte demersimus.

[1] Recte enim tertio mersi estis. . . . Recte enim tertio mersi estis. . . . Illa enim trina immersio typum dominæ exprimit sepulturæ. . . . Semel mergebat in baptismo parvulos. *Summa sentent., Tract* v. cap. 3; *Patrol. Lat.*, vol. 176, p. 130. Migne. Parisiis.

trator of baptism, says: "*You immersed a man,* and said, '*I baptize you in the name of the Father, and of the Son, and of the Holy Spirit;*' and you say to me, ' This man is a Christian. He has been baptized in the name of the Father, and of the Son, and of the Holy Spirit. *I have immersed him three times in the water*,[1] and I said when I immersed him, *I baptize you in the name of the Father, and of the Son, and of the Holy Spirit.*'"

In the twelfth century immersion was the recognized mode of baptism in Europe and out of it, or such language could not have come from the great writer of St. Victor.

Abelard and Immersion.

Abelard in the twelfth century astonished France, his own country, and all Europe by the splendor of his genius and by the rapidity with which he reached the loftiest heights of fame. This acute reasoner adopts the language of Pope Gregory the Great about baptism as his own, and declares that " In baptism it is of no consequence whether *you immerse the infants once or three times; by three im-*

---

[1] Mersisti hominem. . . . Ego illum mersi tertio in aquam. Ego dixi cum mergerem. . . . *Hugo. de St. Vict., De Sacram.*, lib. ii. pars vi.; *Patrol. Lat.*, vol. 176, p. 443.

mersions the Trinity can be exhibited, and by one the unity of the divinity."[1]

But Abelard did not say, "It is of no consequence in baptism whether you *pour, sprinkle,* or immerse once or three times."

PETER LOMBARD AND IMMERSION.

Lombard was a native of Italy, and at first a student at Bologna. In pursuit of a theological education he came to Paris, where he employed his advantages so successfully that he was appointed a professor of theology and afterward Bishop of Paris. He composed a system of theology based upon the writings of the Fathers, and chiefly from Hilary, Ambrose, Jerome, and Augustine, which was received with enthusiasm throughout Europe, and which became the "text-book of divinity" for some generations. He died A. D. 1164, after wielding for years an influence seldom equalled. Writing of baptism, he says:

"*Baptism is called dipping—that is, the external washing of the body*—administered with a prescribed form of words." Then he approvingly quotes the following from Pope Zachary: "An English synod positively decreed that *any one immersed* without

[1] In baptismate vel ter vel semel mergere, quando tribus mersionibus. *Patrol. Lat.*, vol. 178, p. 1510. Migne. Parisiis.

the invocation of the Trinity had not the sacrament of regeneration, which is undoubtedly true, because if any one *is plunged into the font of baptism* without the invocation of the Trinity, his Christianity is not complete.

"If you inquire *about the immersion*—in what way it ought to be performed—we answer briefly: *Either once or three times, according to the different customs of the Church.*"[1] Lombard then proceeds to quote Gregory's letter to Leander, giving his sanction to trine or single immersion in Spain.

As an authority for the baptismal customs of Western Christendom no man stood before Peter Lombard in the twelfth century.

Dupin, the Church Historian, and Immersion.

This learned Roman Catholic, though writing for his own community, gave the world, in the end of the seventeenth century, the most extensive, exact, and in the main impartial history of the writers of the Christian Church ever penned; and his

---

[1] Baptismus dicitur intinctio . . . sine invocatione Trinitatis mersus fuisset . . . mersus in fontem baptismi. . . . De immersione vero si quæritur . . . vel semel, vel ter pro vario more ecclesiæ. *Sentent. Quatuor.*, lib. iv. dist. iii., 1, 2, 9, vol. 192, pp. 843, 845 ; *Patrol. Lat.* Migne. Parisiis.

record of the movements in and around the Church of Christ is unusually reliable.

Speaking of baptism in the third century, he says: "*They baptized,* with some ceremonies, *those that were well instructed in their religion, and who had given satisfactory signs of their sincere conversion. They generally dipped them thrice in the water.*"[1]

Of the fourth century he says: "Baptism was administered to infants and adults with many ceremonies. *They were dipped three times into the water,*"[2] etc.

Of the thirteenth century he says: "*The triple immersion was still in use.*"[3]

[1] Dupin's *Ecclesiastical History,* i. 589. Dublin, 1723.
[2] *Ibid.,* i. 630.   [3] *Ibid.,* ii. 395.

SPAIN.

St. Isidore and Immersion.

Isidore was the grandson of Theodoric, King of Italy. He was born at Seville in Spain, and after the death of his brother Leander he became bishop of his native city, A. D. 595. Isidore was a man of profound learning for his day, and a prolific writer. He made a deep impression upon his countrymen and the Western nations, which ages did not remove. The Eighth Council of Toledo gives him this commendation: "The excellent doctor of our age, Isidore, the greatest ornament of the Catholic Church, the last of the Fathers with regard to the times, but such as may for his learning be compared to the first, the most learned man of past ages."[1]

Speaking of baptism, Isidore says: "Once it behooves us to be washed for Christ, as Christ has once died for us; for if there is one God and one faith, of necessity also there is one baptism, seeing there is one death of Christ, *into the image of which we are immersed through the mystery of the holy font,*

[1] *Dupin*, ii. 4. Dublin, 1824.

that dying to this world we might be buried with Christ, and that we might be raised up from the same waters in the likeness[1] *of his resurrection.*"

St. Isidore speaks on the mode of baptism as an American Baptist pastor of the nineteenth century.

The Fourth Council of Toledo and Immersion.

This Spanish council was convened by King Sisenand A. D. 633. It was composed of the archbishops of Seville, Narbonne, Braga, Merida, Toledo, and Tarragona, with fifty-three suffragan bishops, and with seven presbyters representing bishops. Many of the orthodox Christians in Spain were very indignant at the change in baptism from trine to single immersion; and neither Pope Gregory's letter nor the authority of their own most venerable bishops was able to silence them. To calm this disturbance and unite the Spanish Catholics the council decreed:

"For, shunning the scandal of schism or the use of an heretical practice, *we observe a single immersion in baptism.* Nor do they *who immerse three times* ap-

[1] In cujus imaginem mergimur per mysterium sacri fontis, ut consepeliamur Christo morientes huic mundo, et ab iisdem aquis in forma resurrectionis ejus emergimur. *De Eccles. Offic., Patrol. Lat.*, vol. 83, p. 821. Migne. Parisiis.

pear to us to approve of the claims of heretics, although they follow their custom [of trine immersion]. And that no one may doubt the propriety of this single sacrament, let him see that in it the death and resurrection of Christ are shown forth. *For the immersion in the waters is a descent, as it were, into the grave; and again the emersion from the waters is a resurrection.* Likewise, he may see displayed in it the unity of the Deity and the Trinity of persons—the unity whilst *we immerse once,* and the Trinity whilst we baptize in the name of the Father, and of the Son, and of the Holy Spirit."[1] The council first quote the letter of Pope Gregory to Leander, which they emphatically commend. Gregory's letter from this time became a celebrated document, to which for centuries there was continual reference to show that either trine or single immersion was orthodox.

This canon of Toledo, with Gregory's letter, is in Labbe and Cossart's *Sacrorum Conciliorum.* The authors of this immense work were learned Jesuits,

[1] Simplicem teneamus baptismi mersionem; ne videantur apud nos, qui tertio mergunt. . . . Nam in aquis mersio, quasi ad infernum descensio est; et rursus ab aquis emersio, resurrectio est . . . unitatem, dum semel mergimus; Trinitatem. . . . *Conc. Tolet.,* iv. can. 5, *Labbe et Cossart.,* vol. x. pp. 614, 615. Florentiæ, 1764.

and nothing supposed to be lacking in Catholic orthodoxy is likely to be found in its pages.

The fifth canon of the Fourth Council of Toledo breathes the spirit of the apostle Paul or of a modern Baptist.

SWEDEN AND DENMARK.

St. Anschar and Scandinavian Immersions.

TILL the ninth century little had been done by Christians for the conversion of the Danes and Swedes. Anschar, though not the first laborer among these hardy Pagans, obtained such a measure of well-deserved success that he is justly called "the apostle of the Scandinavians." He was born A. D. 801; he was educated in the monastery of Corbie in France, of which he became a monk, and he died A. D. 865, having been a legate of the pope and the first archbishop of Hamburg. He was a true successor of the heroic band chosen by the Teacher of Nazareth to carry his gospel over the nations. The leader of an enterprise which was so successfully started, and which, under the labors of his successors, became everywhere triumphant, was honored as a canonized saint among the Swedes and Danes, and as a bishop worthy of the love of Christendom.

His biography was written in prose by his companion Rimbertus, and in a poetic form by Gualdo, a monk of Corbie in the eleventh century. These two works were published in Stockholm in 1677, in Latin, under the title of *The Double Life of St. Anschar*. Peter Lambecius, an eminent scholar, wrote notes for *The Double Life*. Claudius Arrhenius, professor of history in the great Swedish University of Upsala, added some contributions to the work. Gualdo, describing the success of Anschar in the time of King Horicus [Eric], relates that "both sexes hastened *to be immersed in the sacred waters*."[1] And again: "When the king had accomplished what he wished, he called the saint to himself, and he gave him liberty to build churches throughout the region, to have priests with him, *and to immerse freely all who wished* [baptism] *in the liquid waters*."[2]

Commenting on *The Double Life*, and especially on the conduct of some of Anschar's converts who wanted to defer baptism till near death, that its waters might wash away all their sins just as they were about to enter heaven, the learned Lambecius says:

"They who delay baptism for this reason are not

---

[1] Sexus uterque sacris mergi properabat in undis. *St. Anscharii Vita Gemina*, p. 195. Holmiæ, 1677.

[2] Qui vellent, liquidis mersare licenter in undis. *Ibid.*, p. 202.

so censurable as those who put it off as long as possible through bashfulness and shame; since formerly men and women, laying aside their bashfulness, their whole bodies being entirely nude, were baptized in the presence of all; and that *not by sprinkling indeed, but by immersion or sinking them.*" [1]

Poppo, an honored missionary among the Danes, was so highly esteemed, according to Neander, that many places were named after him—such as Poppholz, a forest between Flensburg and Schleswig, where, as tradition relates, he built himself a hut. "*In a brook which flows by the spot, Hillegenbach, he is said to have baptized his disciples.*" [2] No climate for ages was too cold for the Saviour's enjoined immersion.

[1] Non per aspersionem scilicet, sed per immersionem, seu καταδυσιν. *St. Anscharii Vita Gemina,* p. 255. Holmiæ, 1677.

[2] Neander's *History of the Christian Religion and Church,* vol. iii. p. 289. Boston, 1869.

GERMANY.

Baptisms by St. Boniface, the Apostle of the Germans.

St. Boniface, whose proper name was Winfrid, was born in Devonshire, in England, in 680. When he was thirty years of age he was filled with enthusiasm to preach Christ to the heathen, and soon after he assisted the aged Willibrord, Archbishop of Utrecht, in spreading the gospel among the Pagan Frieslanders for three years. Afterward he came to Upper Hesse as a missionary. There, in the presence of a great multitude of idolaters, he cut down an ancient oak consecrated for ages to Jupiter. In its fall the tree, instead of killing him, broke into four pieces, and the daring Boniface denounced the absurdity and wickedness of worshipping such an idol. Hosts of Pagans forthwith gave up their false gods and were baptized as Christians.

Othlon, one of the biographers of Boniface, was a German monk of the eleventh century. His *Life, Letters, and Sermons of St. Boniface* is an excellent work.

Gregory the Second was chiefly remarkable for exacting an oath of obedience to the pope from the first German bishop—an act of wrong which is now universal in the Papal Church.

Pope Zacharias, whose letter to Boniface on baptism is so explicit, was a prelate of signal ability, and his opinions on the initiatory sacrament of the Christian Church were those accepted by all Roman Catholics in his day.

Othlon, in his life of Boniface, after speaking of his great success in Frisia, says: "There also he entered other parts of Germany that he might preach. He went to the Hessians located on the confines of the Saxons, whom in like manner he converted in large numbers from Paganism, and *he washed many thousands of men in* the sacrament of baptism."[1] This was one of the largest baptisms that ever occurred, and the solemn rite was administered by immersion. The word *wash* is never employed to describe sprinkling or pouring in baptism. Garments are washed by dipping.

---

[1] Tunc etiam alias Germaniæ partes prædicandi causa adiit, Hessones videlicet in Saxonum confinio positos. Quos cum similiter a paganicæ superstitionis cultu magna ex parte converteret, multaque millia hominum baptismatis sacramento abluisset. *St. Bonifac. Mogunt. Archiepisc.*, *Vita*, cap. 12; *Script. Ecclesiast.*, viii. sæc. Migne. Parisiis, 1863.

Pope Gregory the Second, in a letter to the German clergy and laity commending Boniface, uses the same word to describe his baptism. "Some persons," says he, "who had no knowledge of God or of holy baptism, *were washed*[1] in water"—that is, *bathed* in water.

Pope Zacharias, in a letter to Boniface showing the need of baptism and of invoking the Trinity in administering it, with special reference to the error of an Irish presbyter in Germany named Samson, who taught that a man might be made a Christian without *the bath* of regeneration and without the invocation of the Trinity, says: "Whosoever has been *washed* without the invocation of the Trinity has not the sacrament of regeneration [baptism], as it is assuredly true that if any one has been *immersed* in the baptismal fountain without the invocation of the Trinity, he has not been made perfect until he shall have been baptized in the name of the Father, and of the Son, and of the Holy Spirit. . . . Whosoever is *immersed*, the Trinity being invoked in gospel language after the rule laid down by the Lord, in the name of the Father, and of the Son, and of the Holy Spirit, has that sacrament without doubt. . . . But

[1] Aliquos vero, qui nec Dei cognitionem habentes, nec baptismatis sacri unda sunt loti. *Ep. III., Gregor. Papæ II. Script. Ecclesiast.*, viii. sæc. p. 501. Migne. Parisiis, 1863.

about those *who immerse in the fountain of baptism* without the invocation of the Trinity, it is known to thy fraternity that the series of sacred rules contains something which we advise you to hold tenaciously: 'Be ye holy, as I also am holy.'"[1] Here there is no difficulty about the mode of baptism between the errorists of that day and the pope. It was immersion in both cases. The evil which Zacharias sought to banish was the rejection of the names of the Trinity in the administration of baptism. The baptism, which he first calls washing, he describes as immersion three times afterward.

Boniface had taken a solemn oath to obey Gregory the Second and his successors. In it he swears:

[1] Quicunque sine invocatione Trinitatis lotus fuisset, sacramentum regenerationis non haberet. Quod omnino verum est, quia si mersus in fonte baptismatis quis fuit sine invocatione Trinitatis perfectus non est, nisi fuerit in nomine Patris, et Filii, et Spiritus Sancti baptizatus . . . si evangelicis quis verbis, invocata Trinitate, juxta regulam a Domino positam, quicunque mersus esset in nomina Patris, et Filii, et Spiritus Sancti, quod sacramentum sine dubio haberet. . . . Sed de his qui sine invocatione Trinitatis mergunt in fonte baptismatis, fraternitati tuæ notum est quid de illis sacrorum canonum series continet, quod et tenere te firmiter hortamur. . . . Sancti estote, quoniam et ego sanctus sum. *Zach. Papæ, Ep. XI., ad Bonif. Archiepisc.*, pp. 943, 994; *Script. Ecclesiast.*, viii. sæc. Migne, 1863.

"I, Boniface, bishop by the grace of God, will render to you, blessed Peter, the chief of the apostles, and to thy vicar, the blessed Pope Gregory, *and his successors, allegiance in everything*,[1] and the purity of the holy catholic faith; and I will abide in *the unity* of the same faith, by the help of God." This was a new oath, voluntarily taken by Boniface, which he carried out to the letter in everything; and there can be no doubt of his strict compliance with Zacharias's baptismal instructions in the immersion of candidates as well as in the sacred names invoked in the celebration of the ordinance.

Trine immersion was universal among his countrymen in England, and those of them who left their country as missionaries *buried* the baptized *in the waters*. Willibrord, the honored predecessor of Boniface in one of his continental mission-fields, and one of his own countrymen, who had the great Alcuin for his biographer, was once in an island called Fositeland, from its god, Fosite; and in that island, according to Alcuin, there was a fountain which boiled up, the water of which no one might presume to drink unless he did it secretly, because it was dedicated to the god. Alcuin declares that

[1] Omnem fidem . . . in unitate ejusdem fidei Deo operante persistere. *Jurament. quo S. Bonifac., Script. Eccles.*, viii. sæc. Migne. Parisiis, 1863.

"Willibrord *baptized three men in that fountain*, with the invocation of the holy Trinity."[1] The baptism took place in a fountain boiling up from bubbling springs and overflowing its sides.

Immersion was the baptism of Willibrord of England and of Zacharias, whom Boniface was bound by a solemn oath to obey in religion in everything; and Boniface administered immersion to the hundred thousand converts whom he baptized in Germany.

ALCUIN ON IMMERSION.

This distinguished Englishman was a graduate, and subsequently the principal, of the celebrated school at York, at that time the chief seat of learning in Western Europe. He wrote freely and correctly in Latin, and he was familiar with Greek and Hebrew. He revised the Latin Vulgate, and presented it to Charlemagne. He taught astronomy, philosophy, rhetoric, mathematics, and theology in the court of Charlemagne, and he founded schools throughout the vast empire of that monarch at his expense and under his patronage. He wielded an influence over the emperor and Europe, over churches, states, and seats of learning, greater than

---

[1] Tres homines in eo fonte cum invocatione sanctæ Trinitatis baptizavit. *Vita St. Willibrordi, Patrol. Lat.*, vol. 101, p. 700. Migne. Parisiis.

any other man who lived in the eighth century. His religious opinions were in perfect harmony with the doctrines held by Christians in England, France, Germany, and Italy. He is therefore a first-rate witness for the general practices of baptism in his times.

TRINE IMMERSION.

In a learned letter to the canons of Lyons he says:

"Spain, formerly the nurse of tyrants, is now the nurse of schismatics. There, *contrary to the universal*[1] *custom of the holy Church of God, a doubt in regard to baptism has been proclaimed.* Certain persons affirm that *there should be one immersion* [only], *performed with* the invocation of the Trinity. The apostle seems to differ from that doctrine where he says, 'For ye are buried with Christ by baptism.' Rom. vi. 4. And though this is to be understood figuratively, yet we know that Christ was three days

---

[1] Universalem sanctæ Dei ecclesiæ consuetudinem . . . affirmantes quidam sub invocatione Trinitatis unam esse mersionem agendam. . . . Possunt tres noctes tres mersiones, et tres dies elevationes designare . . . in nomine sanctæ Trinitatis trina submersione baptizatur . . . epistolam vero quam a beato Gregorio de simpla mersione dicunt esse conscriptam. *Alcuini Epistolæ*, Ep. 90; *Patrol. Lat.*, vol. 100, pp. 289–293. Migne. Parisiis.

and three nights in the sepulchre. . . . The *three nights may signify three immersions, and the three days thrice lifting up from*" [the water]. He correctly quotes St. Jerome, St. Ambrose, and Pope Leo the Great *to prove that they administered baptism by trine immersion.* " *This testimony,*" says he, "*was left to us by the chief teachers and most holy Fathers.*" He then appeals to the baptismal usages known to the canons of Lyons: "The Pagan becomes one of the catechumens. He renounces Satan and all his hurtful pomps, etc., and in the name of the holy Trinity *he is baptized by trine immersion.*" This is Alcuin's baptism, and the baptism of all Christians East and West when he wrote, except some Roman Catholics in Spain, who gave but one immersion in baptism. Alcuin proceeds to notice a letter of Pope Gregory the Great to Leander, a Spanish bishop, written in the end of the sixth century, in which he approves of *a toleration for a single immersion in that country*, for certain reasons which he gives; and Alcuin declares that " he did not find that letter in the book of his epistles which was brought to him from Rome, . . . and he doubted whether it was written by Gregory or by some founder of that party."

Alcuin had considerable reason for doubting the genuineness of Gregory's letter, for he knew that all Europe, and all Christians outside of it, observed one baptism in three immersions, except some Spaniards who administered one immersion; and this doubt of such a man as Alcuin about the authenticity of Gregory's letter is a strong proof of the "*universal custom*," as he calls it, of "trine immersion." If immersion, once or thrice, or pouring or sprinkling, were all usual and held in equal esteem, why does the most intelligent man of the age send to Rome for Gregory's *Book of Epistles* to see if the pope had written a letter tolerating one immersion in Spain and exacting three elsewhere? It was a long and costly and dangerous journey to Rome, and it is clear that Alcuin recognized no baptism but trine immersion, or he would never have sent to Rome on such a business; and he believed there should be no other in Spain than the plungings practised in all other countries.

And when Alcuin failed to find the letter among Gregory's *Epistles*, he concluded that it must be a forgery, as no pope could set aside the trine immersion administered in all the churches for ages.

But Gregory did write the letter, and kept no copy of it. Leander received and preserved it. The same thing happened to other epistles of the same pope, copies of which were not in his *Book of Epistles* in Alcuin's time.

It would have amazed Alcuin to have seen the work of a descendant of one of his adopted German fellow-citizens, had he been able to look down the ages, and to have read in it that his imperial patron "Charles sufficiently experienced how little durable was the conversion of the Saxons, when at his command *hundreds at the same moment stepped into a river* and had water poured over them in sign of baptism."[1] Alcuin saw these Saxons baptized on several occasions; and if he had given an account of what he witnessed, he would have described them as being driven into the river, and as having been immersed three times, and he would not have uttered a word about pouring, for Alcuin was a writer of strict veracity.

On another occasion Alcuin writes about baptism:

"In the name of the holy Trinity a *man is baptized by trine immersion*, and he who was made for an image of the sacred Trinity, by the invocation of the holy Trinity is directly restored to the same image."[2]

In a treatise *On the Divine Offices* Alcuin writes of baptism:

[1] Kohlrausch's *History of Germany*, p. 97. New York. 1870.

[2] Trina submersione. *Alcuini de Baptismi Cæremoniis, Patrol. Lat.*, vol. 101, p. 614. Migne. Parisiis.

"Then the priest *baptizes the infant by trine immersion,* invoking the holy Trinity only once, and speaking thus: 'I baptize[1] you in the name of the Father,' *and he immerses him once;* 'and of the Son,' and he *immerses him again;* 'and of the Holy Spirit,' and *he immerses him* a third time." Such is the testimony of Alcuin—the Dr. Francis Wayland of the eighth century—about the mode of baptism in his day.

Descriptions of Immersion sent to Charlemagne at his own Request by Two of his Bishops.

In the works of Charles the Great the following accounts of baptism are given by two of his prelates:

"What the Greeks call *baptism* [baptism is a Greek word] *is called immersion by the Latins. The infant is immersed three times in the holy font, that triple immersion may figuratively exhibit the three days' burial of Christ. The lifting up from the waters is a likeness of Christ rising from the grave."* [2]

---

[1] Deinde baptizat eum sacerdos sub trina mersione . . . ego te baptizo in nomine Patris, et mergat semel; et Filii, et mergat iterum; et Spiritus Sancti, et mergat tertio. *De Divi Offic.,* cap. 19; *Patrolog. Lat.,* vol. 101, p. 1219. Migne. Parisiis.

[2] Latine tinctio dicitur, infans ter mergitur in sacro fonte ut sepulturam triduanam Christi trina demersio mystice de-

The second writes: "Thus a man made for an image of the Holy Trinity, *dipped by trine immersion* in the name of the Father, and of the Son, and of the Holy Spirit, is restored to the image of the same Trinity."[1]

RABANUS MAURUS ON IMMERSION.

This distinguished man, after presiding over the great abbey of Fulda for twenty years, and founding a seminary for the education of clergymen, which sent forth many able ministers, became Archbishop of Mentz in 847. His conspicuous abilities as a teacher and writer placed him at the head of the German bishops, and conferred honor upon his great instructor, Alcuin. Treating of baptism, he says:

"After these things the fountain is consecrated, and the candidate draws near to baptism itself; and thus in the name of the holy Trinity *he is baptized by trine immersion;* . . . *baptism ought therefore to be conferred by trine immersion with the invocation of the holy Trinity.*"[2]

signaret, et ab aquis elevatio Christi resurgentis instar est de sepulcro. *Carolus Magnus*, ii. p. 940. Migne. Parisiis, 1862.

[1] Trina submersione tinctus. *Ibid.*, p. 938.

[2] Trina submersione baptizatur . . . oportet ergo cum invocatione Sanctæ Trinitatis sub trina mersione baptismum confici. *Lib. de Sacr. Ordin.*, cap. 14; *Patrol. Lat.*, vol. 112, p. 1175. Migne. Parisiis.

HAYMO, BISHOP OF HALBERSTADT, ON IMMERSION.

Haymo was a disciple of Alcuin. He flourished about the middle of the ninth century. He was the intimate friend of Rabanus Maurus. Commenting on Romans vi. 4, he says of Christ:

"He himself arose on the third day alive, and we, *after a third immersion, shall arise to life from the death of sins.*"[1]

WILAFRID STRABO (OR STRABUS) AND IMMERSION.

This author was a German abbot who lived in the ninth century. He wrote in prose and poetry, and his works possess learning and merit. Of baptism he says:

"In the beginning believers were *freely baptized in rivers or fountains.* Our Lord Jesus Christ himself, to consecrate the same laver for us, was *baptized* by John *in the Jordan.* And we read elsewhere that John was baptizing in Enon near Salim, because there was much water there. And Philip the evangelist baptized the eunuch *in a fountain which he found by the way.*

---

[1] Post ternam mersionem resurgemus de morte. *Expos. in Epist. ad Rom., Patrol. Lat.*, vol. 117, p. 412. Migne. Parisiis.

"*Some want trine immersion*, because of its resemblance to the three days' burial [of Christ], and because the *Apostolic Canons and the custom of the Romans* required it.[1]

"*Others contended for a single immersion to exhibit the unity of the Godhead.*" Strabo then refers to the controversy in the Fourth Council of Toledo about trine and single immersion, and to the letter of Pope Gregory the Great advising the Spaniards to practise one immersion for the sake of their Arian neighbors, though declaring that the Romans administered baptism with three immersions. He then adds: "It is to be noticed that *many were baptized, not only by immersion,* but by pouring water over them; and *if there was any necessity*[2] baptism could still be administered in that way; as in the Passion of the blessed Laurence we read that a certain person was baptized from a pitcher brought in. This was customary when the height of very tall persons would not permit them to be dipped in small baptisteries."

[1] Primo simplicitur in fluviis vel fontibus baptizatos credentes. . . . Alii trinam immersionem volunt . . . et Romanorum consuetudo observat.

[2] Alii unam propter divinitatis unitatem contendunt . . . non solem mergendo, verum etiam desuper fundendo . . . si necessitas sit. *De Rebus Eccles., Patrol. Lat.,* vol. 114, pp. 957-959. Migne. Parisiis.

St. Laurence was martyred about A. D. 258, and the work in which Strabo read the story of the man whom Laurence baptized by pouring—*The Acts of St. Laurence*—is notoriously mixed with falsehoods,[1] and can gather no authority from the fact that Strabo quoted it, for sacred forgeries were alarmingly numerous long before his day. And as the practice of immersion in baptism in the time of St. Laurence was universal except in the case of a handful of *Clinics*—so small that they scarcely deserve to be named—the story is unworthy of notice. Strabo appeals to no occurrence of pouring in his day except *in case of necessity*. Immersion, trine or single, was the baptism of Christendom.

REGINO ON IMMERSION.

Regino was Abbot of Prum, in the diocese of Treves, in the end of the ninth and in the beginning of the tenth century. He was regarded as an author of some standing in his own times, and men who love to examine the writings of the distant past still read Abbot Regino. In his work on *Ecclesiastical Discipline* he says:

"*Those whom we baptize we immerse three times;*

[1] Wall's *History of Infant Baptism*, part ii. chap. ix. 2, p. 710. Nashville, 1860.

and we instruct them to renounce in words Satan and his angels."[1]

St. Bruno and Immersion.

Bruno in the eleventh century was twelve years Bishop of Würtzburg. He was Duke of Carinthia, but preferred the service of God to the pursuits which generally engaged nobles. He wrote expositions of the ancient creeds and of the Psalms. Commenting upon the word "deluge" in one of the Psalms, he says:

"Here *deluge* signifies *baptism*, or the *waters of baptism*, through which a man is purified, as the world was cleansed by the Deluge."[2]

According to St. Bruno, baptism covers the baptized person with water just as completely as the Deluge covered the earth. Of the completeness of its submersion there can be no question.

Immersions in Pomerania.

Otto, Bishop of Bamberg, in the year 1124 was

[1] Ter mergimus quos baptizamus. *De Eccles. Dis., Patrol. Lat.*, vol. 132, p. 338. Migne. Parisiis.

[2] Hic significat diluvium baptismum sive aquas baptismi. *Expos. Psal., Patrologiæ Lat.*, vol. 142, p. 129. Migne. Parisiis.

preaching as a missionary in Pomerania, and in Pyritz he gathered a large body of converts. "Seven days," says Neander, "were spent by the bishop in giving instruction. Three days were appointed for spiritual and bodily preparation to receive the ordinance of baptism. They held a fast and bathed themselves, that they might with cleanliness and decency submit to the sacred ordinance. *Large vessels filled with water were sunk in the ground and surrounded with curtains. Behind these baptism was administered, in the form customary at that period, by immersion.* During their twenty days' residence in this town *seven thousand were baptized*, and the persons baptized were instructed in the matters contained in the confession of faith and respecting the most important acts of worship."[1]

Rupert on Immersion.

Rupert, Abbot of Deutz, in Germany, on the banks of the Rhine, opposite Cologne, in the twelfth century, was an author of great industry. But of his numerous works his commentary on almost the entire Scriptures is best known. He speaks of baptism in the following terms:

---

[1] Neander's *History of the Christian Religion and Church,* vol. vi. p. 8. Boston, 1865.

"Otherwise why *by trine immersion are we baptized in the name of the Father, and of the Son, and of the Holy Spirit?*" [1]

LUTHER AND IMMERSION.

The great German Reformer, who rendered harmless the thunders of the Vatican and inflicted blows upon the Papacy from which it will never recover, speaks strongly in favor of immersion. In his essay *On the Sacrament of Baptism* he begins with the following:

"First, baptism is a Greek word. In Latin it can be translated *immersion, as when we plunge something into water that it may be completely covered with water;* and although that custom has been given up by most persons, for they do not wholly submerge the children, but only pour on a little water, *yet they ought to be completely immersed and straightway drawn out.*" [2] Such is the testimony of one of the greatest

---

[1] Alioqué cur sub trina mersione baptizamur? . . . *Trin. et Oper., Patrol. Lat.*, vol. 167, p. 1034. Migne. Parisiis.

[2] Primo nomen baptismus Græcum est; Latine potest verti mersio, cum immergimus aliquid in aquam, ut totum tegatur aqua. Et quamvis ille mos jam aboleverit apud plerosque (neque enim totos demergunt pueros, sed tantum paucula aqua perfundunt) debebant tamen prorsus immergi, et statim retrahi. . . . *De Sacram. Bapt., Opera Lutheri*, vol. i. fol. p. 319, 1564.

instruments ever used by Jehovah to extend the empire of truth.

Counsel and Advice of Dr. Martin Luther to a Minister [as to] how a Jewess [a Virgin] is to be Baptized. Anno, 1530.

[Translated from the German by the Rev. J. S. Gubelmann, Philadelphia.]

"Grace and peace in the Lord: It is not necessary, dear pastor, to remind you that you are first, for a time, diligently to instruct the person who is to be baptized regarding the sum of the Ten Commandments, of the Christian faith [creed or confession], and of the Lord's Prayer; also concerning what baptism is, what it benefits and signifies.

"But as regards the [her] public baptism, I am content that, covered with a cloth (as women in the bath), she shall sit in a tub, with the water reaching to the neck,[1] clad with the bathing-cloth, and that she shall be three times dipped with the head into the water[2] by the baptizer, with the usual words—namely, 'I baptize thee in the name of the Father, and of the Son, and of the Holy Ghost. Amen.' . . .

"The dead also are clad with a white garment or winding-sheet, thereby to remind us of our baptism,

[1] Im Wasser bis an den Hals reichend.
[2] Mit dem Haupt dreimal ins Wasser getaucht würde.

by which we are with Christ buried into death, etc. By both, by baptism and by death, the resurrection of the dead is signified and expressed, as baptism itself is nothing else than a passage through death into the future eternal life.

"You may also give to her my greeting in Christ and service of Christian love. Farewell in the Lord. From my solitude. Anno MDXXX."[1]

In Luther's small *Catechism,* Halle edition, printed and published by Christoph Salfeld's Wittwe und Erben [widow and heirs of Christoph Salfeld] in the year 1713, the following passage occurs in the appendix to the *Catechism,*[2] added to give instruction and direction concerning baptism:

"Do you wish to be baptized? Yes.

"Thereupon let him take the infant and *dip*[3] it into the baptism,[4] saying, 'I baptize thee in the name of the Father, and of the Son, and of the Holy Ghost.'"

[1] *Luther's Works,* 1560 (in 8 folio volumes), vol. i., p. 183.

[2] Anhang oder Taufbüchlein.

[3] The word here used by Luther, "tauchen," cannot possibly mean anything else than "to dip," as all who understand the German language will grant. J. S. G.

[4] *Tauche* es in die Taufe.

SWITZERLAND.

John Calvin and Immersion.

The Reformer of Geneva possessed a penetrating and powerful intellect, an extensive and accurate acquaintance with the divine word, the ancient Fathers, and the beliefs and practices of Christians of all ages, and a royal influence over a multitude of believers in many lands and generations.

The apostle Paul, Augustine of Hippo, and John Calvin were three of the mightiest ministers ever commissioned by the Saviour. Of baptism Calvin writes:

"And that he as truly and certainly performs these things internally on our souls as we see that *our bodies are externally washed, submerged, and enclosed in water*" [when baptized].[1] Again:

"Whether the baptized person is wholly *immersed*, and that *three times or once*, or whether water is only poured or sprinkled upon him, is of no consequence. In that matter churches ought to be free,

---

[1] Videmus corpus nostrum extra ablui, submergi, circumdari. *Instit. Christ. Relig.*, lib. iv. cap. 15, sec. 14, p. 641. London, 1576.

according to the difference of countries. *The very word baptize, however, signifies to immerse; and it is certain that immersion was observed by the ancient Church.*" [1]

Our Presbyterian brethren in this country, the direct followers of Calvin, refuse the liberty of baptizing by single or trine immersion, as well as by pouring or sprinkling, as we have lately noticed in their disapproval of the immersion administered by the Rev. Mr. Clark, one of their ministers in this State.

As the very word *baptize* means *to immerse*, and as *it is certain that the ancient Church immersed the baptized, according to Calvin,* how is it that a sturdy Presbyterian like Calvin should license any change?

---

[1] Quanquam et ipsum baptizandi verbum mergere significat, et mergendi ritum veteri ecclesiæ observatum fuisse constat. *Instit. Christ. Relig.* lib. iv. cap. 15, sec. 19, p. 644. London, 1576.

ITALY.

Clinic Baptisms, or Baptisms "for Death" and Baptism "for Life" in the Primitive Church.

MANY of the early Christians after the days of the apostles fell into the pestilent heresy that by baptism their sins were remitted; and while they universally and earnestly insisted that immersion was the only baptism for *the living and healthy,* yet to secure forgiveness through baptism *for the dying* they created two other baptisms. The *first* was pouring water all over a dying man who could not be immersed, so that he was as completely drenched with it as if he had been plunged in it. This baptism was regarded *with toleration* for the dying only. If a man recovered from threatened death, his baptism was regarded *as defective,* and it disqualified him from ministerial service except under certain conditions. Dr. Cave, the Episcopalian author of *Primitive Christianity,* says of clinic baptism—that is, the baptism of those who were *in their beds* through disease—that "it was accounted *a less solemn and perfect kind of baptism,* partly because it was done, *not by immersion*, but by sprinkling—partly because persons were supposed at such a time to desire it chiefly out of a fear of death."[1]

The historian Eusebius says: "It was not lawful to promote one baptized by pouring on his sick bed to any order of the clergy."[2] And while occasionally favoritism or necessity might set this order aside, yet for a great while the stigma of a vital defect rested upon couch baptism if the diseased person was restored.

Eusebius quotes with approval a description of clinic baptism by Cornelius, Bishop of Rome, in which he expresses doubts about the validity of Novatian's baptism, who was "poured around" in a time of sickness, and he adds, "If, indeed, it be proper to say that one like him did receive baptism." The Council of Neo-Cæsarea in its twelfth canon decreed that "if any man was baptized only in time of sickness, he shall not be ordained a presbyter, because his faith was not voluntary, unless his subsequent faith and diligence recommend him, or else the scarcity of men makes it necessary to ordain him."[3] Chrysostom doubted the salvation of such men. "They receive baptism," says

[1] Cave's *Primitive Christianity*, p. 150. Oxford, 1840.
[2] *Eccles. Hist.*, vi. 43, p. 244. Parisiis, 1659.
[3] Bingham's *Antiquities*, book iv. chap. 3, sec. 11.

he, "lying upon their beds, you receive it in the bosom of the Church. They receive it weeping, and you with joy. They with groans, and you with thanksgiving. While the sacrament is administered children cry, the wife tears her hair, friends are dejected, servants weep, the whole house is in mourning; and if you observe the spirit of the sick person you shall find it more full of sorrow than that of the bystanders."[1] Chrysostom's[2] idea of a sick-bed baptism is the opinion we entertain of the death-bed repentance of one whom God had often called, but whose ears were stopped until he felt that he was just stepping into his presence, and then, while terror was his master, he would be baptized somehow, giving a sorrowful illustration of the doctrine that "conscience doth make cowards of us all."

These sick-bed professors on their recovery were greeted with sneers, and their piety subjected to merriment. The clergy sometimes had to appeal to Christians to treat them as brethren, and not as slaves driven to make a profession of faith through fear. It was common to call them "*Clin-*

[1] *Dupin*, i. p. 319. Dublin, 1773.

[2] This article is placed with *Italian* descriptions of baptism and baptisms, because Novatian, the most notorious clinic of all time, was a Roman presbyter.

ics," instead of *Christians*. The word means literally a bed, and as applied to those baptized on their couches it contained the idea that they were ailing disciples, professors from fright, sick-bed servants of God, who were not likely to honor him in health. Cyprian is indignant at these reproaches, and gives utterance to his feelings in these words: "As to the nickname which some have thought fit to fix upon those who have thus [by baptism on their beds] obtained the grace of Christ through his saving water and through faith in him, and their calling such persons *Clinics* instead of *Christians*, I am at a loss to find out the original of this appellation," etc.[1]

But clinic baptism never spread, and the number of times when it occurred is very much smaller than is commonly supposed. It could only exist, even to a limited extent, when believers' baptism was the custom of Christians, when a host of men like Constantine the Great and Ambrose and Augustine, with Christian principles, remained unbaptized after reaching adult or mature years. As infant baptism became general, the candidate never put off baptism through shame or fear, or to have all his sins washed out just before entering heaven; and as a consequence clinic baptism declined, and

---

[1] *Ep. 76, ad Magnum*, pp. 121, 122. Coloniæ, 1607.

was limited to dying babes. But a brand marked clinic baptism as long as it existed.

More than a century after Novatian had his memorable baptism by "pouring around," Socrates, the historian, tells us that a Jew had been confined to his bed by paralysis, and had been benefited neither by medical skill nor by the prayers of his Jewish brethren, and that he determined to have recourse to Christian baptism.

Atticus, the Archbishop of Constantinople, instructed him in the first principles of Christian truth, and preached to him the hope in Christ, and then, instead of going to his bed and pouring water around him, he directed him to be brought in his bed to the font. And the paralytic Jew receiving baptism with a sincere faith, as soon as he was *taken out of the water* found himself perfectly cured of his disease.[1] In the *Centuriæ Magdeburgenses* it is said of this convert, "*He was brought, together with his bed, to the baptistery, and he was let down into the sacred font, and* on the completion of the rite *he was lifted up again from it.*"[2] This baptism occurred at the capital of the empire and of the intelligence of the Eastern world, and it is clear

[1] *Eccles. Hist.*, vii. 4.

[2] In sacrum lavacrum demissus, et, peracto ritu, inde rursum levatus. *Centu. Magde.*, iv p. 576. Norimburgæ, 1765.

testimony that even the paralyzed shunned *pouring around* for baptism, and that such an act was only "the forlorn hope" of the dying—an act which should be carefully avoided by all who wanted obedience without serious defects.

Martyrdom was *the second baptism* for the *departing*. If a man, without baptism in water, died by the persecutions of the Saviour's enemies because he loved Jesus, he was regarded by the primitive Christians as baptized; and his baptism in his own blood, it was universally understood, would wash away his sins. Cyprian says of unbaptized catechumens who were slain for Jesus' sake: "These were not deprived of the sacrament of baptism, since they were baptized in the most glorious and powerful baptism of their own blood."[1] But this was a baptism for the grave, and valid only if the man departed. If he recovered after being half or two-thirds martyred, he must be immersed in water to have his sins forgiven.

The ancient Christians, after the apostles, had two baptisms for those going into eternity—*profuse* pouring and martyrdom. If the man recovered, the first was regarded as defective; the second could only have value when completed by death. *But for those in health there was but one baptism, and*

[1] *Cypr. Ep. 73, ad Jub.*, p. 108. Coloniæ, 1607.

it was the complete immersion of the whole body in water.

Justin Martyr and Immersion.

The reputation of this sufferer for Jesus as a man of intelligence and as a believer of undoubted piety has always stood high in the Church of Christ. Treating of baptism, he writes:

"As many as are persuaded and believe that the things which we teach and declare are true, and promise that they are determined to live accordingly, are taught to pray to God, and to beseech him with fasting to grant them remission for their past sins, while we also pray and fast with them. *We then lead them to a place where there is water,*[1] *and there they are regenerated in the same manner as we also were; for they are then washed in that water* in the name of God, the Father and Lord of the universe, and of our Saviour Jesus Christ, and of the Holy Spirit." This is Professor Coleman's translation.[2] He makes the following comment upon the

---

[1] Ἔπειτα ἄγονται ὑφ' ἡμῶν ἔνθα ὕδωρ ἐστι . . . τὸ ἐν τῷ ὕδατι τότε λουτρὸν ποιοῦνται. *Just. Philos. et Mart., Apol. I. Pro Christ., Patrologia Græca,* vol. vi. p. 240. Migne. Parisiis, 1857.

[2] *Ancient Christianity Exemplified,* p. 271. Philadelphia, 1852.

statement of Justin in another part of his work: "Justin Martyr gives us the first and intelligible account of a Christian baptism [after the New Testament]. The conducting of the candidate *to a place where there is water,* and then baptizing him, instead of causing water to be brought, seems to intimate that at this time the Eastern Church, or at least the Church of Ephesus, *had begun to baptize by immersion.*"[1] Dr. Coleman gives his views with a frankness which Justin's simple words in the original Greek would naturally inspire. The renowned martyr and apologist for Christianity, like his Master, the Son of Mary, was an immersionist beyond a doubt.

AMBROSE, BISHOP OF MILAN, ON BAPTISM.

The world has had many greater but few better men than St. Ambrose. He entered a church in Milan as governor to quiet a violent controversy about a successor to Auxentius, the dead Arian bishop. While in the sacred edifice he was unanimously proclaimed bishop, though not yet baptized. He accepted the office, and he discharged its duties in a spirit of fearless fidelity, and he lived to stand among the first bishops in the Christian world. In

[1] Coleman's *Ancient Christianity Exemplified,* p. 368. Philadelphia, 1852.

the little work he wrote—*On the Sacraments*—he says to a baptized person:

"Thou wast asked, Dost thou believe in God, the omnipotent Father? and thou saidst, I believe; *and thou wast immersed*—that is, *thou wast buried.* Again thou wast asked, Dost thou believe in our Lord Jesus Christ and in his cross? and thou saidst, I believe; and *thou wast immersed,* and *therefore thou wast buried with Christ,* for he who is buried with Christ shall rise with Christ. A third time thou wast asked, Dost thou believe in the Holy Spirit? and thou saidst, I believe; and a third time *thou wast immersed;* . . . for when thou *dost immerse,* thou dost form a likeness of death and burial."[1] Ambrose uses the language of Paul as correctly as if he had been a Baptist.

Pope Leo the Great and Immersion.

Leo became Pope of Rome A. D. 440. Like Gregory VII. and Innocent III., he was endowed with splendid talents. In any position in human society, and in any age of earthly history, Leo would have shone as a star of the first magnitude.

[1] Mersisti, hoc est, sepultus es, . . . et mersisti, ideo et Christo es consepultus: qui enim Christo consepelitur cum Christo resurgit, . . . tertio mersisti . . . cum enim mergis, mortis suscipis et sepulturæ similitudinem. *De Sacramentis,* lib. iv. 7; *Patrol. Lat.,* vol. 16, p. 448. Migne. Parisiis.

Nothing of importance to the interests of Christendom during his pontificate was effected without his powerful assistance. He gave the see of Rome more help in her efforts to secure the mastery of Christ's Church than any of his predecessors. Few of the popes have had "*Great*" added to their names, and few of them have deserved it; but Leo's shining abilities justly earned this title. Speaking of baptism, he says:

"*Trine immersion is an imitation of the three days' burial [of Christ], and the elevation from the waters is a figure [of the Saviour] rising from the grave.*"[1] These words of Leo were used for centuries by the Church teachers of the Old World, as the Nicene Creed was quoted as a general expression of orthodoxy.

St. Maximus, Bishop of Turin, and Immersion.

This prelate was the author of sixty-three homilies that have come down to our times. Though not a man of remarkable ability, he possessed an unusual amount of piety. His works were published in Paris, with the writings of Pope Leo the

[1] Sepulturam triduanam imitatur trina demersio, et ab aquis elevatio, resurgentis instar est de sepulcro. *Ep. 16 St. Leo. Mag., Patrol. Lat.*, vol. 54, p. 699. Migne. Parisiis.

Great, in 1623. He was Bishop of Turin in the latter part of the fifth century. Of baptism and of the baptized he writes:

"*After you promised to believe we plunged your bodies three times in the sacred fountain.* This order of baptism is observed to express a double mystery; *for ye are rightly immersed three times* who have been baptized in the name of Jesus Christ, who arose on the third day from the dead; *for this immersion, thrice repeated, is a figure of our Lord's burial, through which ye are buried with Christ in baptism, that ye may rise again with Christ in faith;* that, washed from sins, you may live by imitating Christ in the sanctity of virtues." [1]

Arator's Description of Baptism.

Arator was born in Italy, and flourished from A. D. 527 to A. D. 544. He followed for a time the legal profession, then he became an officer in the palace of King Athalaric. Pope Vigilius made him a subdeacon of the Church of Rome.

In his poetical account of the facts recorded in

[1] Tertio corpora vestra in sacro fonte demersimus. . . . Recte enim tertio mersi estis. Illa enim tertio repetita demersio . . . per quam Christo consepulti estis in baptismo. S. Maxim. Episc. Tauren., De Bap., Patrol. Lat., vol. 57, p. 778. Migne. Parisiis.

the Acts of the Apostles, speaking of the Pentecostal converts, he says:

"The Shepherd multiplied the sheep, and *he washed* not less than three thousand of the common people *in the river of the Lamb* on that day. Here first by the command of God the practice of baptism arose."[1]

Speaking of the baptism of the eunuch, he writes: "The abounding faith of the eunuch began hastily to burn for the *waters in sight; and, immersed in the gulf*, he laid aside the burden of the serpent."[2]

POPE GREGORY THE GREAT AND IMMERSION.

Gregory the Great was chosen pope at the end of the sixth century. He honestly and earnestly tried to be relieved of the responsibility and honor of the Roman see, but he did not succeed; and his modesty greatly increased his popularity. The success of his mission to the Pagan English extended his fame among all Christian nations. He was warm-hearted and sincerely religious; he was sometimes

---

[1] Flumina deluit Agni . . . baptismatis usus exoritur. *De Actibus Apostol.*, lib. i. 77; *Patrol. Lat.*, vol. 68, p. 114. Migne. Parisiis.

[2] Conspectis properanter aquis . . . gurgite mersus. *Ibid.*, lib. i. 132; vol. 68, p. 152.

tyrannical and superstitious; he was modest and he was meddlesome; he was great in zeal, in shrewdness, and in the estimation of all Christians; he was for a few years the most influential man in Christendom. No pope was ever more venerated than the first of the Gregories. Of baptism this pope writes:

"*The body is immersed*, the soul is washed."[1] This declaration is clear enough about immersion, and no hint is given that pouring or sprinkling will do as well.

When Gregory became pope the Arians in Spain were numerous and annoying. Like Christians in all other lands, they had three immersions in baptism, and they said that the immersion in the name of the Father, coming first, showed that the Father was above the Son and the Spirit—that the second and the third immersions were but inferior honors for persons subordinate to the Father. This argument against the divinity of the Son and of the Spirit was extensively used, and it was felt by many to be very powerful. To oppose this heresy some of the orthodox conceived the idea of having but one immersion in the three sacred names, which must bestow undivided and equal honor upon each person in the

---

[1] Corpus intingitur, anima abluitur. *Gregor. Mag.*, tom. v.; *Patrol. Lat.*, vol. 79, p. 493. Migne. Parisiis.

Trinity. One immersion, however, was considered an innovation, and many denounced it as if it were not baptism, just as a man's arm is not the man. To obtain the assistance of Gregory's great popularity, Leander, Bishop of Seville, the leading prelate of Spain, wrote for the pope's opinion on the disputed question. Gregory sent a reply, from which we quote:

"About the *three immersions in baptism*, no one could answer more truly than you yourself have judged. *We immerse*[1] *three times*, to show the mystery of the three days' burial, and that the infant drawn out of the waters may show forth the resurrection on the third day. But if any one thinks that this is done for veneration of the exalted Trinity, immersing but once in the waters in baptizing brings no opposition to that, because whilst in three subsistences there is one substance, there will be no fault in immersing once or *three times, since in three*

[1] De trina mersione baptismatis nil responderi verius potest quam sensisti. Nos autem quod tertio mergimus triduanæ sepulturæ sacramenta signamus, ut dum tertio infans ab aquis educitur, resurrectio triduani temporis exprematur . . . reprehensible esse nullatenus potest infantem in baptismate vel ter, vel semel mergere, quando et in tribus mersionibus personarum trinitas, et in una potest divinitatis singularitas designari. *Gregor. Mag.*, tom. iii. ep. 43, *ad Leand.; Patrol. Lat.,* vol. 77, pp. 497, 498. Migne. Parisiis.

immersions the trinity of persons can be represented, and in one the unity of the Godhead. But because now, even by heretics, *the infant is immersed three times in baptism,* I think among you it should not be done, lest while we count up *the immersions,* they divide the Godhead."

Gregory was a pontiff of whom Catholics in all ages have been proud, and whom other Christians have regarded with favor. Thoroughly versed in the customs of all Christians, he was competent to testify about the universal mode of baptism. Gregory knew nothing of sprinkling or pouring in baptism. If either had been customary, how easy it would have been to tell Leander, what so many are accustomed to say at the present day, that "*the mode* of baptism was of no account; anything would serve if water was used"! But Gregory only knew of triple or single immersion in baptism.

Maxentius of Aquila and Immersion.

Maxentius owed his exalted ecclesiastical dignity to the special favor of the Emperor Lothaire. He presided over his see in the early part of the ninth century. Of baptism he writes:

"In the name of the holy Trinity *they are baptized by trine immersion,* and the man who was made in the image of the holy Trinity is properly restored to the same image a second time by the invocation of the sacred Trinity."[1]

THE ROMAN CATHLIC CHURCH AND IMMERSION.

A committee appointed by the Council of Trent compiled a system of divinity called the *Catechism of the Council of Trent*, and three years after the dissolution of the council the *Catechism* was given to the world by command of Pope Pius V. In this work it is said:

"Wherefore, baptism by the apostle is called a bath;[2] but the ablution is not rendered more perfect when any one is immersed in water, *although we perceive that this mode was long observed from the earliest times in the Church*, than either by the pouring of water, which we recognize as a frequent practice now, or by sprinkling."[3] The *Catechism* decreed by the Council of Trent and issued by Pope Pius V. declares that immersion was long observed, and that from the earliest times of the Church. No statement could be given by the

[1] Trina submersione baptizatur. *Patrol. Lat.*, vol. 106, p. 57. Migne. Parisiis.

[2] *Vulgate*, Titus iii. 5, per lavacrum regenerationis.

[3] Ablutio autem non magis fit, quum aliquis aqua mergitur, quod diu a primis temporibus in ecclesia observatum animadvertimus. *Catech. Conc. Trident.*, p. 136. Lipsiæ, 1865.

Roman Catholic Church of greater authority on any question than this solemn assurance in regard to the baptism of the early ages.

An Immersion by a Roman Catholic Priest in Milan, witnessed by Howard Malcom, D. D., LL.D.

The doctor writes in 1875:

"When I was visiting portions of Europe in 1830, I went to Milan in Italy to see the Duomo, or cathedral, second only to St. Peter's in Rome. While surveying the vast interior I noticed a small party entering the principal door. They proceeded to something at one side which looked like a high-post bedstead with crimson curtains. As they approached it, it was rolled out on wheels, and I saw that it was a beautiful baptistery made of marble, holding water about four feet deep, and of the size used in America for adult baptisms.

"I approached the party, which stood at one side, while a handsome priest stood at the other. When he had recited the appointed liturgy, he stretched out his hands toward one of the babes. The lady standing by the nurse unfastened its dress at the neck, and with one skilful effort removed all its clothing, leaving it wrapped round and round with a swaddling-cloth from head to foot. The priest received

Baptism of the Ages.

BAPTISTERY IN THE CATHEDRAL AT MILAN.

Page 150.

it, and taking his place at the side of the font, *he carefully lowered the child into the water*, with the appropriate form of words. I stood at the end of the baptistery, and not one of the little ones made any outcry, and of course they could not kick.

"As the party was dispersing I respectfully approached the priest and inquired if he spoke French. He answered in the affirmative. I then told him that I admired his form and his skill in baptizing children—that I was an ecclesiastic from America, and that I was not aware that the Church of Rome practised immersion. He said *that immersion was the only mode of baptism at the beginning*, and it continued till the Roman hierarchy in the third century [it was many centuries later] introduced sprinkling; but Milan continued the original practice till that time."

As Dr. A. P. Stanley, Dean of Westminster, London, declares:

"With the two exceptions of the *Cathedral of Milan* and the sect of the Baptists, a few drops of water are now *the Western substitute for the threefold plunge into the rushing rivers or the wide baptisteries of the East.*" [1]

[1] Stanley's *History of the Eastern Church*, p. 117. New York, 1870.

The Baptistery of St. John de Lateran, and an Ancient Baptism annually Administered in it.

The Rev. A. J. Rowland, pastor of the Tenth Baptist Church, Philadelphia, has at our request kindly furnished us with the following account of the Lateran baptistery and pool:

"I visited the baptistery of St. John Lateran, in Rome, on Sunday afternoon, Sept. 24, 1876. The building is octagonal in form, and stands a little distance from the fine old church which gives it its name. One is struck immediately on approaching with the antiquity of its appearance, and is not surprised to learn from the guide that it dates back to the time of Constantine, and that in this very building the first Christian emperor of Rome was baptized, A. D. 337. The building is about fifty feet in diameter. The pool of the baptistery is of green basalt, and it is about twenty feet long by fifteen wide, the form being that of an ellipse. There seemed to be a false wooden floor in the bottom, but the *depth even with this was something over three feet.* I asked the 'cicerone' who showed us the place, who seemed to belong to one of the lower orders of the clergy, the meaning of this large font, so unlike those in modern churches, and he replied that its size was due to *the fact that anciently people were immersed.* I inquired if it was ever used for immersion now. 'Yes,' he said; '*on Easter Eve Jews and Pagans who accept the faith of the Church are baptized here in that way.*' This fact I subsequently found also in Bædeker's celebrated guide-book.

"On the right and left of the baptistery building doors open into two small apartments, now known as oratorios or chapels; on the ceiling of one of them is an old mosaic, dating back to the fifth century, representing John the Baptist *performing the rite of immersion.* It struck me that these two apartments may have been originally dressing-rooms for baptismal occasions. Between the font and the outer walls there is space enough, I think, for four or five hundred spectators to witness a baptism. On the day of my visit this space was occupied in part by a number of classes of boys who were taught by Romish priests very much after the fashion of our Sunday-schools.

"Altogether, the building proclaims in the most positive way the antiquity of the practice of immersion. It seems absurd to suppose that the ancient Church would have gone to the trouble of erecting this large building for no other purpose than to immerse its members, had not this been the primitive and prescribed mode. I left the building with my faith in baptism by immersion deeply confirmed and strengthened."

The baptismal service in this church at Easter was in full exercise a thousand years ago; and the mode was immersion and the time Easter.[1] The pope administered baptism in the font of St. John de Lateran, wearing "a pair of waxed drawers"—that is, waterproof drawers.

[1] *History of Baptism,* by Robinson, p. 106. Nashville, 1860.

RUSSIA.

The Baptism of Vladimir the Great, Prince of Russia, and of the People of Kieff.

Vladimir, the ruler of the Russians in A. D. 988, was a fierce warrior and conqueror, and guilty of a licentiousness unsurpassed by sultans or Solomons. He was as heartless a despot and tyrant as ever trod on human rights and bleeding hearts. He was also a furious idolater, and would not scruple to offer human sacrifices to his abominable god. He made a new statue of Perune, his deity, with a silver head, which he placed near his palace. He waged war on the city of Kherson, the ruins of which still exist near Sevastopol, that he might compel the Greek emperors, its sovereigns, to give him their sister Anna in marriage, and through some exalted ecclesiastic to confer Christian baptism upon him. He captured the city, and the fair princess became his wife, to the grief or deliverance of nearly a thousand women whom he forthwith dismissed.

Kelly, in his *History of Russia*, describes the

baptisms following the capture of Kherson: "Vladimir," says he, "listened to some catechetical lectures, received the rite of baptism and the name of Basil, and restored to his brothers-in-law the conquests he had recently made.

"He had Perune tied to the tail of a horse on his return to Kieff, dragged to the Borysthenes, and all the way twelve stout soldiers, with great cudgels, beat the deified log, which was afterward thrown into the river.

"At Kieff, one day, he issued a proclamation ordering all the inhabitants to repair the next morning *to the banks of the river to be baptized, which they joyfully obeyed.*"[1]

The Immersion at Kieff, according to Dean Stanley.

"*The whole people of Kieff,*" says he, "*were immersed in the Dnieper,* some sitting on the banks, some plunged in, others swimming, while the priests read the prayers. The spot was consecrated by the first Christian church, and Kieff henceforward became the Canterbury of the Russian empire."[2]

---

[1] Kelly's *History of Russia*, pp. 32, 33. Bohn, London, 1854.

[2] Stanley's *History of the Eastern Church*, p. 409. New York, 1870.

MOURAVIEFF'S ACCOUNT OF THE BAPTISMS AFTER THE CAPTURE OF KHERSON.

Mouravieff in 1842 was chamberlain to the Emperor of Russia, and "under-procurator of the most holy governing synod," St. Petersburg, 1838. The Rev. R. W. Blackmore, an Episcopalian chaplain in Cronstadt, who translated Mouravieff's work, says: "He gives a clear, succinct, and regular account of the events which marked the introduction and progress of Christianity in his native country."[1]

Mouravieff himself says: "On the arrival of the Princess Anna at Kherson, she induced Vladimir to hasten his baptism, for it was so ordered by the wisdom of God that the sight of the prince was at that time much affected by a complaint of the eyes; but at the moment that the Bishop of Kherson laid his hands upon him, *when he had risen up out of the bath of regeneration* [baptism], Vladimir suddenly received not only spiritual illumination, but also the bodily sight of his eyes.

"Vladimir made a proclamation to the people, 'That whoever, on the morrow, should not repair to *the river*, whether rich or poor, he should hold him for his enemy.' At the call of their respected

[1] Mouravieff's *History of the Church of Russia*, Preface, p. 10.

lord all the multitude of the citizens in troops, with their wives and children, *flocked to the Dnieper, and without any manner of opposition received holy baptism as a nation* from the Greek bishops and priests" [who came with Vladimir from Kherson].

"Nestor," says Mouravieff, "draws a touching picture of this baptism of a whole people at once. *Some stood in the water up to their necks, others up to their breasts, holding their young children in their arms; the priests read the prayers from the shore,* naming at once whole companies by the same name. He who was the means of thus bringing them to salvation, filled with a transport of joy at the affecting sight, cried out to the Lord, offering and commending into his hands himself and his people: 'O great God, who hast made heaven and earth, look down upon these thy new people. Grant them, O Lord, to know thee, the true God, as thou hast been made known to Christian lands, and confirm in them a true and unfailing faith; and assist me, O Lord, against my enemy that opposes me, that, trusting in thee and in thy power, I may overcome all his wiles.'"[1]

This baptism of a whole city *in the river Dnieper* was the grand commencement of the triumph of

[1] Mouravieff's *History of the Church of Russia*, pp. 13, 15. Oxford, 1842.

Christianity throughout Russia. Many *thousands were immersed* in the Dnieper at this time, and immersion has been ever since, and is to-day, the only baptism of the Russians. There is a note in Mouravieff on this great baptism in the Dnieper, which states: "The archdeacon who accompanied Macarius, Patriarch of Jerusalem, into Antioch in the time of Nikon *gives a very similar description of the baptism of a whole tribe at once*, of which he himself and the patriarch were witnesses."[1]

The Synod of Vladimir in Russia, and Trine Immersion.

In A. D. 1274, Cyril, the Metropolitan of Kieff, called a synod at Vladimir to restore the discipline of the Church, and among other regulations "it forbade the practice *of using affusion instead of trine immersion in holy baptism*, which was probably creeping into our churches through Galich from the West."[2] This decree will be found in Mouravieff.

A Baptism in the Russian Church, witnessed by Kohl, a German Traveller, about Thirty Years Since.

"As the child, so long as it is unchristened, is a little heathen, and as such a subject of the Evil

[1] Mouravieff's *History of the Church of Russia*, p. 354. Oxford, 1842.   [2] *Ibid.*, p. 48.

Spirit, the priest's first address to it is a demand that it will renounce him. As the child does not answer, the godfathers do so for him, and then the priest spits behind him, and all those present follow his example: they spit at the retreating devil! This is the first act of the baptism. As an interlude, the priest offers up a prayer, and if he has brought singers with him, they sing. During this time the child is in a neutral condition, and it is in fact hard to say to which kingdom his soul belongs. The evil spirits have left him, but the good have not yet taken possession. Before the *immersion* the whole party, preceded by the priest and the godfathers, make a solemn procession around the font. This is repeated three times—in the name of the Father, the Son, and the Holy Ghost. Then the priest consecrates the water and puts a metal cross in it, and afterward *immerses the child* three times, again in the three sacred names, and lastly pronounces the baptismal names bestowed on him. After *the third immersion* the child is a Christian, as the visible sign of which the priest suspends a metal cross to the neck by a black string, and this is kept on the breast as an amulet through life. It is then dressed, the procession around the font repeated, the godfather carrying the child instead of the godmother. Burning tapers are carried before them, whose flame is always supposed to symbolize the Holy Ghost in the Russian Church; they must not begin to flame, therefore, till the child is supposed to be filled with that Spirit. The child is then anointed on the body, eyes, ears, mouth, hands, and feet. Lastly, from four places on its little head the priest cuts crosswise a piece of its silky hair. This is rolled up sometimes with a little wax into a ball and thrown into the font."[1]

THE GREAT DISSENTING COMMUNITY OF STAROVERS, OR OLD BELIEVERS, IN RUSSIA, PRACTISE IMMERSION.

This denomination numbers about eight millions, who have an almost idolatrous regard for ancient national customs and religious observances and peculiarities. They regard the smoking of tobacco as a sin of such unusual magnitude that the drinking of brandy in comparison is a trivial offence. Their converts from the Established Church are solemnly rebaptized. Dean Stanley describes one of their villages which lies "beyond the uttermost barrier of Moscow," called Preobajensk, or the Transfiguration, and according to him its people are industrious, commercial, and in many cases wealthy. "*A straggling lake,*" he says, "extends

[1] *Russia*, by J. G. Kohl, pp. 251, 252. London, 1842.

itself right and left into the village, *in which the Starovers baptize those who come over to them from the Established Church."* [1]

CONVERTS OF ADULT YEARS ARE IMMERSED IN THE RUSSIAN CHURCH.

In the February number of *Harper's Magazine* for 1869 there is a woodcut representing an immersion, as above. (Plate IV.)

The traveller who witnessed it says: "About fifty versts from Nijne Novgorod the population of a large village was gathered in Sunday dress upon the ice. A baptism was in progress, and as we drove past the assemblage I caught a glimpse of a man *plunging through a freshly-cut hole.* Half a minute later he emerged from the crowd and ran toward the nearest house, the water dripping from his garments and hair." [2] The plate from which our picture is taken was furnished to us by the proprietors of *Harper's Magazine*.

[1] Stanley's *History of the Eastern Church*, pp. 509, 511, 515. New York, 1870.

[2] *Harper's Magazine*, vol. 38, p. 300.

Baptism of the Ages.

BAPTISM IN RUSSIA.

Page 162.

TURKEY AND GREECE.

THE GREEK CHURCH.

"THE CONSTITUTIONS AND CANONS OF THE HOLY APOSTLES."

THIS work is divided into eight books, the last one of which ends with the eighty-five Canons.

The entire work is full of Scripture quotations, and while it occasionally teaches error it is rich in precious truths. It is of great antiquity; nearly all its latest parts come but a short way into the fourth century, and its earliest portions stretch up almost to the first. The whole work treats of doctrines, the rights and duties of the clergy, and the principles that should govern all Christians.

In canon twenty-two[1] it condemns all deeds like the one known as "the heroic act of Origen." This canon must have been adopted when the excitement against the fanaticism of Origen was at its height.

Canon six: "Let not a bishop, presbyter, or

[1] *Constitutions and Canons of the Holy Apostles.* New York, 1848.

deacon cast off his own wife under pretence of piety; but if he cast her off, let him be suspended. If he continue to do it let him be deposed."[1] At the Council of Nice, A. D. 325, the spirit of celibacy had so intensified and extended itself that only Paphnutius, an Egyptian bishop brought up in a community of monks and held in the greatest reverence, saved the clergy from the disruption of their families.

The Constitutions expressly declare that a life of "virginity [in monks or nuns] is not commanded by the Lord; the practice is a voluntary one, and must not be used to the reproach of marriage."[2] This decree is as old as the end of the second century.

It gives advice repeatedly to Christians about the proper course to pursue in persecutions, showing that it was written before Constantine the Great crushed his Pagan and persecuting enemies. Whatever these "Constitutions and Canons" lack of the inspired authority claimed for them, and for ages freely accorded to them by multitudes, no competent scholar ever doubted the correctness of the account which they give of the government, discipline, and practices of the churches.

[1] *Constitutions and Canons of the Holy Apostles*, lib. i. cap. 11. New York, 1848.
[2] *Ibid.*, lib. viii. Const. 24.

THE BAPTISM OF THE CONSTITUTIONS AND CANONS.

"He who is to be *initiated into Christ's death* ought first to fast, and then be baptized, for it is not reasonable that he who has been *buried* with Christ and is risen again with him should appear dejected at his very resurrection." [1]

"Thou, therefore, O bishop, according to that type, shalt anoint the head of those that are to be baptized, whether they be men or women, with the holy oil, for a type of the spiritual baptism. Then, either thou, O bishop, or a presbyter under thee, shall pronounce over them the sacred name of the Father, and of the Son, and of the Holy Spirit, and shall *dip them in the water.* And let a deacon receive the man, and a deaconess the woman, that so the conferring of this invaluable seal may be done with a becoming decency." [2]

"If any bishop or presbyter *shall not perform three immersions of one mystery, but shall immerse once in baptism, which is given into the death of the Lord, let him be deposed."* [3] This is the version of this section

[1] *Constitutions and Canons of the Holy Apostles,* lib. viii. Const. 22. New York, 1848.

[2] *Ibid.,* lib. iii. Const. 16.

[3] 'Εί τις ἐπίσκοπος ἢ πρεσβύτερος, μὴ τρία βαπτισματα μιᾶς μνήσες ἐπιτελέση, αλλ' ἐν βάπτισμα εἰς τον θανατυν του κυριου, καθαιρεισθω. *Harduin Conc. Collec.,* vol. xii. p. 22. Paris, 1715.

of the celebrated fiftieth canon given by Dionysius Exiguus;[1] and it was unquestionably the understood meaning of the canon about trine immersion from the beginning. The Bibliotheca Veterum Patrum renders τρία βαπτισματα, three immersions.[2] And Strabo, in the ninth century, says: "Some want *trine immersion*, because of its resemblance to the three days' burial (of Christ), and because '*The Apostolic Canons and the custom of the Romans required it.*'"[3] "The Constitutions and Canons of the Holy Apostles" enjoyed the highest authority for many centuries in the Church, and they demand trine immersion.

Gregory of Nyssa and Immersion.

Gregory Nyssen was one of the most prominent and popular bishops of the Eastern Church. He wielded a powerful influence in the councils of bishops and in the public affairs of the Eastern Empire. He occupied a conspicuous place in the General Council of Constantinople, A. D. 382, and by its appointment delivered before the council the

[1] Trinam mersionem . . . . semel mergat in baptismate. *Codex Canon. Eccles., Patrol. Lat.*, vol. 67, p. 148. Migne. Parisiis.

[2] Si quis episcopus, aut presbyter, non tres mersiones fecerit, sed unam mersionem. *Biblio. Vet. Patrum*, Gallan, tom iii. 244. Venet., 1767.

[3] See *Wilafrid Strabo*.

funeral oration of Meletius, Patriarch of Antioch. In A. D. 385 he preached in Constantinople the funeral discourse of the Empress Placilla. Speaking of baptism, he says:

"*Coming to* the water, *we hide ourselves in it,* as the Saviour hid himself in the earth." [1] With him baptism *concealed* or *covered* the baptized person with water.

Chrysostom and Immersion.

Chrysostom, the persecuted patriarch, eloquent preacher, and earnest Christian, had a widespread popularity, and a popularity that has journeyed down the ages for fifteen centuries, and is never likely to suffer any abatement. In his day many of the clergy hated him, and for some reason the Empress Eudoxia, who took special charge of Arcadius, her unresisting husband, and of his sceptre, regarded Chrysostom with bitter dislike. Once, through her influence, he was sent into exile, but the threatenings of the people and the persuasive terrors of an alarming earthquake made it necessary to recall him to his church. A silver statue of the empress, standing upon a column of por-

---

[1] Τὸ ὕδωρ ἐρχόμενοι ἐκείνῳ ἑαυτοὺς ἐγκρύπτομεν. *Greg. Nyssen,* tom. iii., *De Bap. Christ.*, vol. xlvi., p. 585; *Patrol. Græca.* Migne. Parisiis, 1858.

phyry, had been placed only the half breadth of the street from the church of St. Sophia. To this statue such honors were paid, and around it such shouting, confusion, and wickedness prevailed, as appeared to Chrysostom to be a disgrace to the temple of Jehovah. In a moment of excitement he denounced the statue and the scenes that were constantly occurring around it. The empress was indignant, and John had to leave the capital of the Eastern Cæsars again. Chrysostom is the grand representative of the Greek Church of the fourth century. Writing of baptism, he says:

"*For we sinking our heads in the water, as if in some grave, the old man is buried; and the whole man, having sunk entirely down, is concealed. Then, we emerging, the new man arises again. For as it is easy for us to be immersed and to emerge, so it is easy for God to bury the old man and bring to light the new. This is done three times.*"[1]

The ancient deacons led the man to be baptized into the fountain up to the neck in the water; and

[1] Καθάπερ γάρ ἐν τινι τάφῳ, τῷ ὕδατι κατα δυόντων ἡμῶν τὰς κεφαλὰς, ὁ παλαιὸς ἄνθρωπος θάπτεται, καί καταδὺς κάτω κρύπτεται ὅλος καθαπαξ. Εἶτα ἀνανενόντων ἡμῶν, ὁ καινὸς ἄνεισι πάλιν. Ὥσπερ γὰρ εὔκολον ἡμιν βαπτίσασθαι καὶ ἀνανεῦσαι. Οὕτως εὔκολον τῷ θεῷ θάψαι τόν ἄνθρωπον τόν παλαιὸν καὶ ἀναδεῖξαι τὸν νέον. Τοῦτον δὲ τοῦτο γίνεται. Chrysos. on John iii. 5, vol. viii. p. 168. Parisiis, 1836.

if the candidate was a woman, the deaconesses placed her in the same situation; and the act of baptism after this consisted simply in sinking the head of the person in the water three times in the name of the Holy Trinity; and in this way, according to Chrysostom, "*the whole man, having sunk entirely down, was concealed.*"

PHILOSTORGIUS AND IMMERSION.

Philostorgius was born in Cappadocia about A. D. 364. He was educated in Constantinople, and it is not known whether he was a lawyer or a religious teacher. He wrote an ecclesiastical history, from the origin of Arianism to A. D. 425, which is lost.

Photius, Patriarch of Constantinople in the latter part of the ninth century, made an abridgment of the work of Philostorgius, which still remains; and in the abridged history Philostorgius says:

"The Eunomians *baptized not with trine immersion, but with one immersion*, baptizing, as they said, into the Lord's death."[1]

The word used by Photius, and most probably by Philostorgius, means *sinking or causing to sink.*

From the way in which Philostorgius expresses it,

---

[1] Καταδυσις. *Philostorg. Eccles Hist. Epito.*, lib. x. cap. 4, p. 523. Parisiis, 1673.

it is clear that all but the Eunomians had trine immersion in baptism in the fourth century.

A Baptism in Athens according to the Rites of the Greek Church.

Bayard Taylor, the well-known traveller, while in Athens, witnessed in a private house the immersion of a child. He says:

"I neglected no opportunity of witnessing the ceremonials of the Greek Church. In the East, the sacraments of the Church have still their ancient significance. The people have made little or no spiritual progress in a thousand years, and many forms which elsewhere are retained by the force of habit—their original meaning having long since been lost sight of—are still imbued with vital principle.

"The parents received us at the door. Everything was in readiness for the ceremony. The priest—a tall, vigorous Macedonian, a married man —and the deacon—a very handsome young fellow, with a dark olive complexion and large languishing eyes—now prepared themselves by putting long embroidered collars over their gowns. They then made an altar of the chest of drawers, by placing upon it a picture of the Virgin, with lighted tapers on either side. Then a small table was brought into the centre of the room as a pedestal for a tall tri-forked wax candle, representing the Trinity. A large brazen urn, the baptismal font, was next carried in; the priest's son, a boy of twelve, put coals and incense into the censer, and the ceremony began. The godfather, who was a venerable old gentleman, took his station in front of the font. Beside him stood the nurse holding the babe, a lively boy of six weeks old. Neither of the parents is allowed to be present during the ceremony.

"After some preliminary chants and crossings, in the latter of which the whole company joined, the priest made the sign of the cross three times over the infant, blowing in its face each time. The object of this was to exorcise and banish from its body the evil spirits which are supposed to be in possession of it up to the moment of baptism. The godfather then took it in his arms, and the Nicene Creed was thrice repeated—once by the deacon, once by the priest's son, and once by the godfather. A short liturgy followed, after which the latter pronounced the child's name—'*Apostolos*'—which he had himself chosen. It is very important that the name should be mentioned to no one, not even to the parents, until the moment of baptism; it must then be spoken for the first time.

"The position of godfather in Greece carries with it a great responsibility. In the two Protestant sects which still retain this beautiful custom it is hardly more than a form, complimentary to the person who receives the office, but no longer carrying with it any real obligation. Among the Greeks, however, it is a relation to which belong legally acknowledged rights and duties, still further protected by all the sanction which the Church can confer. The godfather has not only the privilege of paying all the baptismal expenses and presenting the accustomed mug and spoon, but he stands thenceforth in a spiritual relationship to the family which has all the force of a connection by blood. For instance, he is not allowed to marry into the family within the limits of consanguinity prohibited by the Church, which extend as far as the *ninth* degree, whatever that may be. He also watches over the child with paternal care, and in certain cases his authority transcends even that of the parents. The priest and deacon put on embroidered stoles, rather the worse for wear, and the former rolled up his sleeves. Basins of hot and cold water were poured into the font, and stirred together till a proper temperature was obtained. The water was then consecrated by holding a Bible over it, blowing upon it to expel the demons, dividing it with the hand in the form of a cross nine times—three apiece for each person of the Trinity—and various other mystical ceremonies accompanied with nasal chanting. The censer, now puffing a thick cloud of incense, was swung toward the Virgin, then toward us, and then the other guests in succession, each one acknowledging the compliment by an inclination of the head.

"A bottle of oil was next produced, and underwent the same process of consecration as the water. The priest first poured some of it three times into the font in the form of a cross, and then filled the godfather's hollow hand, which was extended to receive it. The infant, having been meanwhile laid upon the floor and stripped, was taken up like a poor, unconscious, wriggling worm as it was, and anointed by the priest upon the forehead, breast, elbows, knees, palms of the hands, and soles of the feet. Each lubrication was accompanied by an appropriate blessing, until every important part of the body had been redeemed from the evil powers. The godfather then used the child as a towel, wiping his oily hands upon it, after which the priest *placed it*[1] *in the font.*

"The little fellow had been yelling lustily up to this time, but *the bath soothed* and quieted him. With one hand the priest *poured water plentifully on his head*, then lifted him out and *dipped him a second*

[1] None of the italics after this are Bayard Taylor's.

time; but instead of affusion, it was this time *complete immersion. Placing his hand over the child's mouth and nose, he plunged it completely under three times in succession.*

"The Greek Christians skilfully avoid the vexed question of 'sprinkling or immersion,' on which so much breath has been vainly spent, by combining both methods. If a child three times sprinkled and three times dipped is not sufficiently baptized, the ordinance had better be set aside.

"The screaming and half-strangled babe was laid on a warm cloth; and while the nurse dried his body the priest cut four bits of hair from the top of his head—in the form of a cross, of course—and threw them into the font. A gaudy dress of blue and white, with a lace cap, the godfather's gift, was then produced, and the priest proceeded to clothe the child. It was an act of great solemnity, in which each article assumed a spiritual significance. Thus: 'I endow thee with the coat of righteousness,' and on went the coat; 'I crown thee with the cap of grace,' and he put it on; . . . . "[1]

[1] *Travels in Greece and Russia,* by Bayard Taylor, pp. 54-59. New York, 1859.

"Office of Holy Baptism" of the Greek Church, by A. N. Arnold, D. D., Chicago.

"*R. The priest enters, and changing his priestly white robe and sleeves, and touching all the candles, having taken the censer, he goes to the font and incenses it with a circular motion; and having laid aside the censer, worships. Then the deacon says:*
'Bless, O Lord.'

"*R. Then the priest, with a loud voice:*
'Blessed be the kingdom of the Father, and of the Son, and of the Holy Spirit, now and always, and world without end. Amen.'

"*R. The deacon:*
'In peace let us beseech the Lord.'

"*R. The choir:*
'Lord, have mercy! In behalf of the peace that is from above and salvation; in behalf of the peace of the whole world; in behalf of this Holy Family and of those in the faith; in behalf of the sanctification of this water, by the power, and the energy, and the impartation of the Holy Spirit, let us beseech the Lord.'

(Then follow twelve other short prayers, occupying a page of the book, all ending as above: then the following:)

'Help, save, have mercy, and keep us;

Through the all-holy, undefiled, hyper-blessed, our glorious Lady, the Mother of God.'

"*R. And while the deacon is saying these things, the priest says by himself the following prayer secretly.*

(Here follows the prayer, occupying nearly a page.)

"*R. It is necessary to understand that he does not speak aloud, but even the 'amen' he says to himself. Afterward he says this prayer aloud.*

(Here follows a prayer, occupying a whole page, and ending as follows, after a reference to Christ's sanctifying the waters of the Jordan by his baptism:)

' Be thou present, therefore, O merciful King, now also by the impartation of thy Holy Spirit, and sanctify this water.'

"*R. (Repeat three times.)*

' And give to it the grace of redemption, the blessing of the Jordan. Make it a fountain of incorruption, a gift of sanctification, a deliverance from sin, a medicine against diseases, destructive to demons, inaccessible to hostile powers, filled with angelic strength. Let those who plot against thy creature flee from it; because, O Lord, I have invoked thy name, which is wonderful and glorious, and terrible to the adversaries.'

"*R. Then he makes the sign of the cross and breathes upon the water three times, and prays, saying:*

'Let all the hostile powers be shattered under the sign of the venerable cross (three times). Let all the aërial and invisible idols depart, and let there not hide in this water any dark demon; neither let there descend upon the baptized, we beseech thee, any wicked spirit, bringing darkness of thoughts and perturbation of mind. But do thou, O Lord of all, make this water a water of redemption, a water of sanctification, a purification of flesh and spirit, a release from bonds, a remission of transgressions, an enlightenment of souls, a laver of regeneration, a renewal of spirit, a grace of adoption, a garment of incorruption, a fountain of life. For thou, O Lord, hast said, "Wash you, make you clean, put away the wickedness of your souls." Thou hast given to us the regeneration from above, through water and Spirit. Manifest thyself, O Lord, in this, and grant that the one baptized in it may be transformed, so as to put off the old man, which is corrupt according to the deceitful lusts, and may put on the new man, which is renewed after the image of Him that created him, in order that, being planted together in the likeness of his death by baptism, he may become a partaker also of his resurrection, and preserving the gift of the Holy Spirit and increasing the deposit of grace, may receive the prize of the heavenly calling, and be numbered with the firstborn who are registered in heaven, in thee, our God and Lord Jesus Christ. For to thee belong glory, power, honor, and worship, together with thine eternal Father, and thy holy and good and life-giving Spirit, now and always, and world without end. Amen.

'Peace be with all. Bow your heads to the Lord.'

"*R. And he breathes upon the vessel of oil three times, and makes the sign of the cross three times upon the oil, which is held by the deacon; and when the deacon says, 'Let us beseech the Lord,' the priest shall say the following prayer:*

'O Lord God of our fathers, who didst send to those who were in Noah's ark a dove, having a twig of olive in its mouth, a symbol of reconciliation and of salvation from the deluge, and didst foreshadow by these things the mystery of grace, and didst furnish the fruit of the olive tree for the fulfilment of thy holy mysteries, and by this didst fill with the Holy Spirit those under the law, and dost perfect those under grace, do thou bless also this oil, by the power and energy and impartation of thy Holy Spirit, so that it may become an ointment of incorruption, a weapon of righteousness, a renewing of soul and body, an antidote of every diabolical influence, a deliverance from all evils to those anointed in faith, and partaking of it to thy glory, and of thy only-begotten Son, and of thy all-holy and good and life-giving Spirit, now and always, and world without end.'

"*R. The choir, 'Amen.' The deacon, 'Let us give attention.'*
"*R. The priest, singing the hallelujah three times with the people, makes the sign of the cross three times with the oil on the water. Then he says aloud,*

'Blessed be God, who enlightens and sanctifies every man coming into the world, now and always, and world without end.'

"*R. The choir, 'Amen.'*
"*R. And the one to be baptized is brought forward. And the priest takes of the oil, and makes the sign of the cross upon the forehead and the breast and the back, saying,*

'The servant of the Lord [name] is anointed with the oil of gladness, in the name of the Father, and of the Son, and of the Holy Spirit, now and always, and world without end. Amen.'

"*R. And he makes the sign of the cross upon his breast and his back.*
"*R. (Making it) upon his breast, he says:*

'For healing of soul and body.'

"*R. (Making it) upon his ears, he says:*

'For the hearing of faith.'

"*R. (Making it) upon his feet, he says:*

'That his steps may go in thy **ways.**'

"*R. (Making it) upon his hands, he says:*
'Thy hands have made me and fashioned me.'
"*R. And when the whole body has been anointed, the priest baptizes him, holding him in an erect posture, and with his face to the east, and saying,*

'The servant of the Lord [name] is baptized in the name of the Father, amen, and of the Son, amen, and of the Holy Spirit, amen, now and always, and world without end. Amen.'

"*R. At each invocation sinking him and raising him.*
"*R. And after the baptism the priest washes his hands,*
"*R. Singing with the people,*

'Blessed are they whose iniquities are forgiven, and whose sins are covered.'

"*R. And the rest of the psalm three times.*
"*R. And putting on him the vestments, he says:*

'The servant of God [name] is clothed with the robe of righteousness, in the name of the Father, and of the Son, and of the Holy Spirit, now and always, and world without end. Amen.'

"*R. And a short hymn [troparion] is sung.*

'Supply to me a shining robe, O merciful Christ, our God, who clothest thyself with light as with a garment.'

"*R. And after he is clothed the priest prays, saying this prayer:*

'Let us beseech the Lord. Blessed art thou, O Lord God Almighty, the Fountain of blessings, the

Sun of righteousness, who sheddest the light of salvation upon those in darkness, by the appearance of thy only-begotten Son and our God, and who hast given to us, who are unworthy, the blessed purification in the holy water and the divine sanctification in the life-giving anointing, and who hast now been pleased to regenerate thy servant, the one newly enlightened by water and Spirit, and hast given to him the remission of all sins, voluntary and involuntary. Do thou, O most royal and merciful Lord, grant to him also the seal of the gift of thy holy, almighty, and adorable Spirit, and the participation of the holy body and the venerable blood of thy Christ. Keep him in thy sanctification, confirm him in the orthodox faith, deliver him from the wicked one, and from all his devices, and keep his soul in thy saving fear, in purity and righteousness, in order that, pleasing thee in every work and word, he may become a son and heir of thy heavenly kingdom.'

"*R. Aloud.*

'For thou art our God, a God of mercy and salvation, and to thee we ascribe glory, to the Father, and to the Son, and to the Holy Spirit, now and always, and world without end. Amen.'

"*R. And after the prayer he anoints the baptized with the holy ointment, making the sign of the cross upon his forehead, and his eyes, and his nostrils, and his mouth, and both his ears, and his breast, and his hands, and his feet, saying:*

'The seal of the gift of the Holy Spirit. Amen.'

"*R. Then the priest, with the sponsor and the child, make the form of a circle, and we sing:*

'As many of you as were baptized into Christ did put on Christ. Hallelujah!'

"*R. This is done three times; then the text,*

'The Lord is my Light and my Saviour. The Lord is the Defender of my life.'

"*R. The Epistle.*
Romans vi. 3–11.

"*R. Gospel from Matthew xxviii. 16-20.*

"*R. Then the bidding prayer and dismission.*

*   *   *   *   *   *

"*R. After seven days the child is again brought to the church for the* ablution (ἀπόλουσις). *After three short prayers,*

"*R. The priest loosens the child's girdle and garment, and uniting the ends of them, wets them with clean water and* sprinkles (ῥαίνει) *the child, saying:*

'Thou hast been justified, thou hast been enlightened,' etc.

"*R. And taking a new sponge with water, he wipes the child's face, and head, and breast, saying:*

'Thou hast been baptized, thou hast been enlightened, thou hast been anointed, thou hast been sanctified, thou hast been washed in the name of the

Father, and of the Son, and of the Holy Spirit, now and ever, and world without end. Amen.'[1]

"The lines marked *R.* in the margin are the *rubrics*, and are printed in *red* letters in the book.

"The confirmation service is united with the baptismal. The anointing, or chrism, mentioned is the Greek rite of confirmation.

"The short service of ablution is appended, because of the *sprinkling* mentioned in it, which it is supposed may have been mistaken for baptism by some of those not very well informed travellers who have testified so positively that they have seen baptism performed by sprinkling in the Greek Church."

DR. ARNOLD AND IMMERSIONS IN GREECE.

Dr. Arnold—until recently a professor in the Baptist Theological Seminary of Chicago—is one of the most scholarly men in or out of the Baptist denomination in the United States. He was for several years a missionary in Greece, with the most favorable opportunities for becoming familiar with the religious observances of the Greeks. Writing of modern baptism among them, he says:

"The writer has repeatedly seen baptism administered according to the Greek ritual, *and in every instance it has been a triple immersion. If, as may*

[1] Translated from the Εὐχολόγεον, pp. 137–147.

sometimes happen, any little portion of the body is not completely submerged when the child is placed naked in the font, the priest, by a movement of his hand, sends a wave over it." [1]

THE GREEK CHURCH AND IMMERSION.

Dean Stanley, an eminent Episcopalian, makes the following statement:

"There can be no question that the original form of baptism—*the very meaning of the word—was complete immersion in the deep baptismal waters,* and that for at least four centuries *any other form was either unknown or regarded, unless in the case of dangerous illness, as an exceptional, almost a* MONSTROUS, *case.* To this form the *Eastern Church still rigidly adheres,* and the most illustrious and venerable portion of it—that of the Byzantine Empire—*absolutely repudiates and ignores any other mode of administration as essentially invalid."* [2]

"The validity of the baptisms [sprinklings] of the Western Church is to this day denied by the Church of Constantinople." [3]

Dean Stanley might have said that twelve centuries instead of four was the period during which immersion was the baptism of Christendom.

[1] *The Baptist Quarterly*, vol. iv. 1870, p. 83.
[2] Stanley's *History of the Eastern Church*, p. 117. New York, 1870.   [3] *Ibid.*, p. 460.

SERVIA.

A Servian Baptism in 1876.

Milan, Prince of Servia, through the war which his principality lately waged with Turkey and the conflict of 1877 between Russia and the Ottoman Porte, has become well known to the reading world. In 1876 a respectable English[1] paper gave the following account of the baptism of his child:

"The infant son of Prince Milan was baptized at the palace, according to the rites of the Greek Church. He received the name of Milosh. Consul Kartzoff represented the Emperor of Russia as sponsor. There was no godmother. The service is a long one. The infant is stripped naked and *completely immersed in the font.* A collect was sung for the prince, the princess, and the Emperor of Russia. With the exception of M. Kartzoff, all the foreign consuls were in plain clothes. In the evening there was a display of fireworks, but no illumination."

[1] *Deal, Walmer, Dover, and Kentish Telegraph*, Oct. 28, 1876.

TURKEY, PERSIA, AND THE EAST.

A Miraculous Baptism, a. d. 1299.

Matthew of Westminster, in his *Flowers of History*, written in the early part of the fourteenth century, tells a very curious Eastern story. He says:

"Paganus, brother of the great Cassanus, King of the Tartars, loved the daughter of the King of Armenia, who was a Christian; accordingly, he begged the father that the girl might be given to him in marriage; but the King of Armenia would not grant his request unless he laid aside the errors of heathenism and became a Christian. . . . His daughter, wishing to spare the people, voluntarily consented [to the marriage]. Afterward, when they had a child born of the male sex, he was found to be hairy and shaggy like a bear. And when he was brought to his father, he said that he was not his, and immediately ordered him to be burned in the fire. But his mother resisted, and ordered him to be baptized; and immediately, as soon as he had been thrice immersed[1] in the sacred

---

[1] *Flowers of History*, vol ii p. 531. London, 1853.

font all the hairiness fell from the child, and he appeared smooth and the most beautiful of infants."

A Portion of the Nestorian Baptismal Service now in Use.

"The deacons shall bring the children into the baptistery, their earrings, rings, and bracelets having been taken off, and they shall inquire the names to be given to the children, and shall communicate the same to the priest. The deacons shall then bind up their loins, and place their stoles under the vessel containing the oil. And every child who is admitted shall be provided with a napkin to be wrapped in after baptism, which shall be carried by the deacon on his shoulder. . . . Then those present shall carefully and properly anoint all over the person of him whom the priest anointed; and they shall not leave any part of him unanointed. Then they shall take him to the priest standing *by the font*, who shall *place him therein*, with his face to the east; and he *shall dip him therein three times*, saying at the first time, 'A. B., be thou baptized in the name of the Father.' *R.* 'Amen.' The second time: 'In the name of the Son.' *R.* 'Amen.' And at the third time: 'In the name of the Holy Ghost.' *R.* 'Amen.' *In dipping him he shall dip him up to the neck, and then put his hand upon him, so that his head may be submerged.*

Then the priest shall *take him out of the font* and give him to the deacon, who shall wrap him up in a white napkin and commit him to his godfathers. Then his clean clothes shall be put on, but his head must be left bare until the priest shall bind on his head-dress after the last signing."[1]

THE ARMENIANS AND IMMERSION.

The Rev. H. G. O. Dwight—a Congregational missionary in Turkey of great worth and of extensive usefulness—in his work called *Christianity in Turkey*, published in 1854, writes:

"The whole number of Armenians now in the world is estimated at not far from three millions. More than half of these—perhaps two-thirds—are inhabitants of Turkey. Large numbers are found in Russia, especially in the Georgian provinces, and very many also in Persia. They live in various parts of India, and some are found in Burmah and China. Wherever they go they are marked for their enterprise, ability, and intelligence, and it is acknowledged on all hands that they possess the elements of a superior character. In Turkey the principal merchants are Armenians, and nearly all the great bankers of the government; and whatever

---

[1] *The Nestorians and their Rituals*, by Badger, Episcopalian, vol. ii. pp. 207, 208. London, 1852.

arts there are that require peculiar ingenuity and skill, they are almost sure to be in the hands of Armenians. They are the Anglo-Saxons of the East."[1]

Giving an account of their religious rites, Dwight states that

"*Baptism is performed by triple immersion,* also by pouring water *afterward* three times upon the head."[2]

The triple pouring *after baptism has been performed* is a custom in the Greek Church, as will be seen by looking at the closing portion of Dr. Arnold's translation of *The Office of Holy Baptism* of that Church. It takes place seven days after the baptism, and is called the "ablution."

The baptism of the Armenians is a "triple immersion," no matter what additions have been made to it.

[1] *Christianity in Turkey,* pp. 13, 14. London, 1854.
[2] *Ibid.,* p. 11.

PALESTINE.

Jewish Proselyte Baptism.

Dr. John Lightfoot, a member of the Westminster Assembly of Divines that framed the Confession of Faith of our American Presbyterian brethren, a Hebrew scholar of unusual research, represents the baptism of proselytes as ages more ancient than Christ's day, and he gives the following account of the method of performing it:

"They do not baptize a proselyte by night, nor on the Sabbath, nor on a holy day. It is required that three men who are scholars of the wise men be present at the baptism of a proselyte, who may take care that the business be rightly performed, and may briefly instruct the catechumen [candidate].

"As soon as the proselyte grows whole of the wound of circumcision they bring him to baptism, and being placed in the water, they again instruct him in some weightier and in some lighter commands of the Law; which being heard, he plunges himself and comes up, and, behold! he is an Israelite in all things. The women place a woman in the waters up to the neck, and two disciples of the wise men, standing without, instruct her about some lighter precepts of the Law and some weightier, while she in the mean time stands in the waters; and then she plungeth herself, and they, turning away their faces, go out, while she comes up out of the water.

"Now, what that plunging was you may know from those things which Maimonides speaks in Mikvaoth: 'Every person baptized must dip his whole body, now stripped and made naked, at one dipping. And wheresoever in the Law washing of the garments or body is mentioned, it means nothing else than the washing of the whole body; for if any wash himself all over except the very tip of his little finger, he is still in his uncleanness.'"[1] This by some is supposed to be the source of Christian baptism.

JEWISH PROSELYTE BAPTISM BY A LEARNED RABBI NOW OFFICIATING IN A CONGREGATION OF AMERICAN ISRAELITES.

"1. The Mikveh is a rabbinical institution of very ancient date. [*Mikveh*, a bath, a gathering of running waters.]

[1] *Lightfoot's Whole Works*, vol. xi. pp. 59–61. London, 1823.

"2. It must possess dimensions enabling a person of average size to plunge into it, without leaving a particle of the body exposed.

"3. The water must flow from the main source, and not be simply poured into it.

"4. Persons voluntarily joining the Hebrew faith must make an immersion as described above, typical of their having cleansed themselves of erroneous ideas and of having become mentally regenerated." This is a very old and a very complete immersion.

A Jewish friend, of marked intelligence and of literary tastes, says of the writer of the above: "He is one of the purest and noblest followers of God's word that ever lived."

Immersion in the New Testament.

"Then went out to John Jerusalem, and all Judea, and all the region round about Jordan, and *were baptized of him in Jordan*, confessing their sins." Matt. iii. 5, 6.

"Then cometh Jesus from Galilee to *Jordan* unto John to be baptized of him; but John forbade him, saying, I have need to be baptized of thee, and comest thou to me? And Jesus answering said unto him, Suffer it to be so now: for thus it becometh us to fulfil all righteousness. Then he suffered him.

and *Jesus when he was baptized went up straightway out of the water."* Matt. iii. 13-16.

"John did baptize in the wilderness, and preach the baptism of repentance, for the remission of sins; and there went out to him all the land of Judea, and they of Jerusalem, and *were all baptized of him in the river Jordan,* confessing their sins." Mark i. 4, 5.

"And John also *was baptizing* in Enon near to Salim, *because there was much water there."* John iii. 23.

"Therefore *we are buried with him by baptism into death,* that like as Christ was *raised up* from the dead by the glory of the Father, even so we also should *walk in newness of life."* Rom. vi. 4.

"Buried with him in baptism, wherein also ye are risen with him, through the faith of the operation of God." Col. ii. 12.

Matthew says that " Jerusalem, and all Judea were baptized *in Jordan ;"* he says that " when the Saviour was baptized he went up straightway *out of the water."* Mark says that "all the land of Judea, and they of Jerusalem, *were baptized by John in the river Jordan ;"* and the apostle John declares that John the Baptist " was baptizing in Enon near to Salim, *because there was much water there."* These baptisms were undoubted immersions.

Professor Coleman, commenting on the words of Justin Martyr, " We then lead them [candidates for baptism] to a place where there is water," says: "The conducting of the candidate to a place where there is water, and there baptizing him, instead of causing water to be brought, seems to intimate that at this time the Eastern Church, or at least the Church of Ephesus, had begun to baptize by immersion."[1] If the professor is right in his conjecture about the mode of Justin's baptism, then every one baptized in the Jordan or at Enon *was immersed*. And as in the New Testament there was "one Lord, one faith and *one baptism*," it would follow that all baptisms recorded in the New Testament were immersions.

The great Dr. John Lightfoot says of John's baptism: "*That the baptism of John was by plunging the body, after the same manner as the washing of unclean persons and the baptism of proselytes, seems to appear from those things which are related of him—namely, that he 'baptized in Jordan;' that he baptized 'in Enon, because there was much water there,' and that Christ, being baptized, 'came up out of the water,' to which that seems to be parallel* (Acts viii.), '*Philip and the eunuch went down into the water,*'"[1] etc. That Dr. Lightfoot is right to us is certain. And if this statement appeared in some public journal, "On the

[1] Coleman's *Ancient Christianity Exemplified*, p. 368. Philadelphia, 1852.

[2] *Lightfoot's Whole Works*, vol. xi. p 63. London, 1823.

second Sunday in May twenty-five persons were baptized in the Mississippi River at Vicksburg," what person of intelligence would dream that they were sprinkled or had water poured upon them?

St. Jerome and Immersion.

The monk of Palestine, who revised the New Testament of the Latin Vulgate and translated the Old, was a power in the fourth century and for ages afterward. He was learned and pious and crotchety; a troublesome neighbor, yet a blessing to the Church. He makes the following statement about trine immersion:

"And many other things which are observed in the churches claim the authority of the written law for themselves, *as in the font to plunge the head three times under the water.*"[1]

Commenting on "one Lord, one faith, and one baptism," Eph. iv. 5, he asserts that

"*We are immersed three times*, that the one mystery of the Trinity might appear."[2]

---

[1] In lavacro ter caput mergitare. *Aaver. Luciferianos,* tom. iii. p. 63. Basle, 1516.

[2] Ter mergimur. *Ibid.,* tom. ix. p. 109.

NORTH AFRICA.

Tertullian on Baptism.

Tertullian was born in Carthage A. D. 160. He was originally a lawyer, and had become a presbyter of the church in his native city. His style and his temper are stiff. He was so conscientious as to be crotchety. After A. D. 200 he joined the Montanists, who are said to have had an exaggerated opinion about the amount of the Spirit possessed by their founder. Before he became a follower of Montanus he wrote his tract on baptism. Tertullian, during and after his own time, enjoyed the warm regards of Christians, especially of Cyprian, the master-spirit of the Church in North Africa in the third century. Tertullian was a lowly Christian, as his last words in *De Baptismo* show. "Ask," he says, "and ye shall receive; seek, and ye shall find; knock, and it shall be opened unto you; and when you ask, I only pray that you would remember Tertullian the sinner." He was the first Christian writer who used the Latin tongue, and Tertullian composed the first work on baptism ever given to the world by a disciple of Jesus. In his treatise on baptism he says:

"We little fish are *born in the water.*"[1] "It is of *no consequence whether (in baptism) a man is washed in the sea or in a pool, in a river or in a fountain, in a lake or in the channel of a river;* nor *is there any difference between those whom John immersed in the Jordan and those whom Peter immersed in the Tiber."*[2] "The act of baptism itself belongs to the flesh, *because we are immersed in water;*[3] its effect is spiritual, because we are freed from sins." "*Christ himself was immersed in the water.*"[4] "*It is one thing to be sprinkled* or taken unawares by the violence of the sea, *and another to be immersed by the discipline of religion.*"[5] Quoting from Paul's letter to the Corinthians about their controversies his saying that "He was not sent *to immerse* men,

[1] Nos pisciculi . . . in aqua nascimur. *De Baptismo*, cap. 1. Lipsiæ, 1839.

[2] Nulla distinctio est, mari quis an stagno, flumine an fonte, lacu an alveo diluatur. Nec quicquam refert inter eos, quos Joannes in Jordane et quos Petros in Tiberi tinxit. *Ibid.*, cap. 4.

[3] Ipsius baptismi carnalis actus, quod in aqua mergimur. *Ibid.*, cap. 7.

[4] Christus ipse aqua tinguitur. *Ibid.*, cap. 9.

[5] Aliud adspergi vel intercepi violentia maris, aliud tingui disciplina religionis. *Ibid.*, cap. 12.

but to preach," he says that "He should first preach, and then *immerse*. . . . He could lawfully *immerse* who had a right to preach."¹ Elsewhere in his works Tertullian says of baptism: "But first in the church, under the management of the bishop, we bear some testimony that we have renounced the devil and his pomps and angels. Then, answering somewhat more fully than the Lord appointed in the Gospel, *we are immersed three times.*"²

"Our Saviour commanded us to *immerse*³ into the Father, and Son, and Holy Spirit; not into one person, and not once, but three times. At each name *we are immersed*⁴ *into each person.*"

¹ Non ad tinguendum . . . licuit et tinguere. *De Baptismo*, cap. 14.

² Ter mergitamur. *De Corona, Patrol. Lat.*, vol. ii. p. 99. Migne. Parisiis.

³ Ut tinguerunt . . . in personas singulas tinguimur. *Liber ad Prap.*, cap. 26; *Ibid.*, ii. 213.

⁴ Tertullian, in his sixteen duodecimo pages on baptism, uses *tingo* forty-six times in the sense of dipping, and *mergo*, to immerse, *abluo*, to wash, and *lavo*, to bathe, ten times to describe baptismal immersion. *Tingo* and *mergo*, *immergo* and *mergito*, with Tertullian were identical in meaning. He uses *tingo* and *mergito* on this very page and in exactly the same sense. *Tingo* is used in the Vulgate when the rich man cries, "Father Abraham, have compassion upon me, and send Lazarus that he may dip (*intingat*) the tip of his finger into water and cool my tongue." Luke xvi. 24. *Tingo* is used

in Matt. xxvi. 23 and in Mark xiv. 20 to express *dipping*. Hugo of St. Victor (*Summa Sentent.*, tract v. cap. 3; *Patrol. Lat.*, vol. 176, p. 130) quotes Gregory's letter to Leander as if he had said: "There will be no fault in immersing (*tingere*) once or thrice, since in three immersions (*mersionibus*) the Trinity can be represented." With Hugo *tingo* and *mergo* meant, in baptism, the same immersion. Boniface, the apostle of the Germans, uses *tingo* in the same sense. He tells the English Abbess Eadburga about spirits which he saw in a vision, "some of which were dipped (*tingebantur*) as if the whole body were immersed" (*mersare*. *Ep. Bonif.*, 20; *Script. Eccles.*, viii., Saec. Migne. Parisiis). In the beginning of the thirteenth century it lost, like baptize, the idea of mode entirely, and came to be employed as the compilers of the *Catechism of the Council of Trent* (*Catech.*, pars ii. cap. 2, quæst. 17, p. 136. Lipsiæ, 1865) use it when they say: "For those who ought to be initiated by this sacrament are either *plunged into water* (*in aquam merguntur*), or water is poured upon them, or they are *tinged* (*tinguntur*)—that is, baptized—by sprinkling." But for 1000 years in Latin Christian literature *tingo* meant baptism by immersion, and it was used apparently in the first Latin version of the New Testament ever made. Jerome, in his revised New Testament of the Vulgate in the fourth century, transfers baptize in the commission, Matt. xxviii. 19. Tertullian, in *De Baptismo*, cap. 13, in the end of the second century, quotes, most probably from the very earliest Latin translation, the same commission; and "*baptizing* them" is *immersing* them (*tinguentes*).

The Baptism of the Bishops of North Africa, A. D. 256.

In that part of the world as early as the end of the second century Christians were numerous. In the middle of the third century a council was held in Carthage to settle the controversy then raging about rebaptizing heretics. The council was composed of eighty-five bishops.

Each bishop gave his opinion, and Cyprian recorded each declaration and numbered it. He was the leading prelate in the council, and he gives his decision last. Munnulus, Bishop of Girba, was the tenth speaker, and the following is his deliverance, as translated by a learned Episcopalian:[1]

"The true doctrine of our holy mother, the Catholic Church, has always been with us, my brethren, and especially in the article of baptism, *and the trine immersion wherewith it is celebrated,* our Lord having said, 'Go ye and baptize the Gentiles in the name of the Father, and of the Son, and of the Holy Spirit, etc.'"[2] Munnulus then proceeds to repudiate all baptisms administered by persons outside the

---

[1] *St. Cyprian's Works*, translated by Nath. Marshall, LL.B., Vicar of St. Vedastus, London, p. 241. London, 1717.

[2] Vel et maxime baptismatis trinitate. *Cypriani Opera*, Conc. Carth., p. 230. Coloniæ, 1617.

Church. Cyprian breathes no word of dissent from the judgment of Munnulus; and no living man in such a meeting was so likely to relieve his mind as the Bishop of Carthage. Tertullian, sixty years before in Carthage, wrote about baptism: We are *immersed three times;* and Cyprian, when asking for Tertullian's works, was accustomed to say, "Give me my master;" so that an agreement on all great questions existed between the bishop and his master the presbyter. Seventy-five bishops followed Munnulus, and no one of them differed from him.

St. Augustine of Hippo and Immersion.

Augustine was a native of North Africa. His father's name was Patric, and his mother's Monica. Like the mothers of many other great men, Monica possessed remarkable talents, and she was a devoted Christian. For many years she labored unsuccessfully for Augustine's conversion. His education, except in Greek, was respectable, and he became a popular teacher of rhetoric in Carthage, Rome, and Milan. His unconverted life was very immoral, and a considerable part of it was spent among the heretical Manichees. At Milan the discourses of the devout Ambrose led Augustine to the Saviour and to a holy life; and the Epistles of Paul the apostle were peculiarly blessed in shaping his opin ions and guiding his affections. He was baptized by Ambrose at Milan A. D. 387, in the thirty-second year of his age. In A. D. 395 he became Bishop of Hippo; and from that obscure spot the light of Augustine's genius went abroad throughout the whole world. He died A. D. 430.

Augustine for ages was the great Church teacher of Christendom; ecclesiastics of all ages, Reformed, Papal, and Greek, have joyfully taken a place at his feet. John Calvin, and John Knox, and Archbishop Cranmer, and John Gill occupied the very spot on which famous popes and cardinals and doctors knelt before the mighty teacher of Hippo. No prelate, in the Papal chair or out of it, enjoyed the reverence accorded to Augustine for years during the later period of his life. He had some errors and a good many faults, but he was unquestionably at the head of the Christian churches in his day; and he was without a superior, after the apostle of the Gentiles, before and since his day. He writes of baptism as follows, in his sermon on "The Mysteries of Baptism":

"*After you promised to believe we plunged your heads three times in the sacred fountain.* This order of baptism is observed to express a double mystery; *for you have been rightly immersed three times* who have received baptism in the name of the Trinity, and *you have been properly immersed three times* who have received baptism in the name of Jesus Christ, who arose from the dead on the third day ; *for that immersion thrice repeated gives a type of the three days' burial of the Lord*, through which [immersion] ye are buried with Christ in baptism, and with Christ in faith, that, washed from sins, you may live in the sanctity of virtue by imitating Christ. Hence the blessed apostle says, 'Are ye ignorant that they who are baptized in Christ Jesus are baptized in his death? for we are buried with him by baptism into death, that as Christ was raised from the dead by the glory of the Father, so we also should walk in newness of life.'"[1] Such, undoubtedly, were the universal views of the mode of baptism and of its significance in Augustine's day.

Some persons have doubted whether Augustine ever wrote our quotation. But, on the other hand, men of profound learning, like Bingham, the author

[1] Postquam vos credere promisistis tertio capita vestra in sacro fonte demersimus. Qui ordo baptismatis duplici mysterii significatione celebratur. Recte enim tertio mersi estis qui accepistis baptismum in nomine Trinitatis. Recte tertio mersi estis qui accepistis baptismum in nomine Jesus Christi, qui tertio die resurrexit a mortuis. Illa enim tertio repetita demersio typum dominicæ exprimit sepulturæ. Per quam Christo consepulti estis in baptismo. Tom. vi., appendix, *Patrol. Lat.*, vol. 40, pp. 1207, 1208.

of *The Antiquities of the Christian Church,* have unhesitatingly received it as a genuine work of the great teacher of Hippo. The sentiments of the quotation were those of Ambrose, who baptized him, and of Jerome, his correspondent, which appear in this volume, and of the whole of orthodox Christendom at this period.

Baptism of Epidophorus, in Carthage, in the Fifth Century.

In that highly respectable authority, the *Centuriæ Magdeburgenses,* it is written:

"Victor, in the Vandalian persecution, mentions in his third book a certain Epidophorus, who was baptized in Carthage, whom Milrita, a venerable deacon, received as regenerated *from the inside of the font.*"[1] He was in the font, and of course immersed in his baptism, and Milrita received him as one born again from the cavity of the font.

Premasius, Bishop of Adrumeta, on Baptism.

This prelate lived in the sixth century, and presided over a diocese in North Africa. In his commentary, at Rom. vi. 4, he writes:

"So that in this way from sons of perdition we

[1] De alveo fontis generatum. *Centu. Magde.,* iv. p. 573. Norimbergæ, 1765.

are made sons of adoption. We die beforehand to our former nature by a second birth. And whilst *we are immersed* in an element allied to earth [water], *we are buried;* and whilst *we arise from the heart of the font*, we are quickened; and from this the sacrament of baptism is very great; and therefore [Paul] says, 'We are buried with him by baptism into death.'"[1]

[1] Submergimur . . . sepelimur; dum e sinu fontis assurgimus. *Ad Epist. a Rom. Comm., Patrol. Lit.*, vol. 68, p. 444. Migne. Parisiis.

EGYPT.

A Baptism by Athanasius.

The immortal defender of the divinity of the Saviour when a boy baptized some other boys in sport. The story is told by Sozomen,[1] Socrates,[2] and by Dean Stanley, chiefly on the authority of Rufinus. Stanley says:

"Alexander, Bishop of Alexandria, was entertaining his clergy in a tower or lofty house overlooking the expanse of sea beside the Alexandrian harbor. He observed a group of children playing on the edge of the shore, and was struck by the grave appearance of their game. His attendant clergy went, at his orders, to catch the boys and bring them before the bishop, who taxed them with having played at religious ceremonies. At first, like all boys caught at a mischievous game, they denied, but at last confessed that they had been imitating the sacrament of baptism—that one of them had been selected to perform the part of bishop, *and that he had duly dipped them in the sea*

---

[1] Sozomen, lib. ii. cap. 17. [2] Socrates, lib. i. cap. 15.

with all the proper questions and addresses. When Alexander found that these forms had been observed, he determined that the baptism was valid; he himself added the consecrating oil of confirmation, and was so much struck with the knowledge and gravity of the boy-bishop that he took him under his charge. This little boy was Athanasius."[1] Notwithstanding the doubts of some, Dean Stanley is right in saying that " the story has every indication of truth."

The Copts and Immersion.

The Copts number about 150,000. They are the descendants of the ancient Egyptians of Joseph's time, and they form a Christian community to which the Abyssinians belong. Their chief prelate is the Patriarch of Alexandria, whose residence is in Cairo. They regularly choose for the Abyssinians their highest ecclesiastical ruler, called the "Abuna," when the office is vacant. The antiquity of their race and some religious peculiarities make them a remarkable people. The Right Reverend Richard Pococke, Lord Bishop of Ossory, in Ireland, describing their customs, says:

"*At baptism they plunge the child three times into*

---

[1] Stanley's *History of the Eastern Church*, p. 324. New York, 1870.

the water, then confirm it and give it the sacrament."[1] A more recent and unquestionable authority says: "*The Copts baptize by immersion*, and practise unction, exorcism, and auricular confession."[2]

[1] *Compendium of Modern Travels*, vol. ii. p. 30. Dublin, 1757.

[2] *Chambers's Encyclopædia.* Philadelphia, 1870.

ABYSSINIA.

Immersions in Abyssinia, Doubtful and Reliable.

James Bruce, the celebrated Scotch traveller, who visited Abyssinia a little over one hundred years since, and whose descriptions of the country, the people, and their customs have been so frequently confirmed in our own times, gives an account of the baptismal rites of the Abyssinians. In this part of his work he quotes the narrative of a sort of annual commemoration of the Saviour's baptism, published by Alvarez, chaplain to the Portuguese embassy under Don Rodrigo de Lima, which reads:

"Before the pond a scaffold was built, covered around with planks, within which sat the king looking toward the pond, his face covered with blue taffeta, while an old man, who was the king's tutor, was standing in the water up to the shoulders, naked as he was born, and half dead with cold, for it had frozen violently in the night. All those that came near him *he took by the head and plunged them in the water*, whether men or women, saying in his own language, 'I baptize you in the name of the Father, Son, and Holy Spirit.'"[1]

Bruce advances a number of plausible reasons why the account of Alvarez should be discredited. We have no desire to take sides in the controversy between the two travellers. If Alvarez tells the truth, the baptism he describes is a *baptism by immersion*. If he is indebted to a fertile imagination for his facts, his story shows that he knew well how an Abyssinian baptism should be performed, as we shall presently see. He would not have represented a mass of his own countrymen as being baptized in his day by plunging them in a pond.

BAPTISMS SEEN BY BRUCE HIMSELF.

"But this I can bear witness of," says our intelligent traveller, "that at no time when I was present—and *I have been present above a hundred times at the baptisms of both adults and infants*, ay, *and of apostates too*—and I never heard other words pronounced than the orthodox baptismal ones, 'I baptize you in the name of the Father, of the Son, and of the Holy Ghost,' *immerging the child in pure water*, into which they first pour a small quantity of oil of olives in the form of a cross."[1] Immerging is only

[1] *Bruce's Travels*, vol. iii. pp. 667, 668. Dublin, 1791.
[2] *Ibid.*, vol. iii. p. 663.

an older English form of the Latin word *immergo,* to immerse, as the poet says:

> " Ye dying sons of men,
> Immerged in sin and woe "—

that is, overwhelmed, immersed, in sin and woe.

No one acquainted with Bruce's perspicacity and veracity would doubt his account of an occurrence which he saw but once, and still less would he hesitate to believe his description of an event which he had seen "above a hundred times;" and so many times Bruce had seen persons *immerged* in Abyssinia when baptized. In one of his journeys he writes: "At half-past eight we began a gradual descent, at first easily enough, till we crossed the small brook Maitemquet, or *the water of baptism.*"[1]

When a brook or creek is called *the water of baptism,* it must refer to immersion as the mode of that baptism from which its name is derived.

[1] *Bruce's Travels,* vol. iii. p. 488. Dublin, 1791.

CONCLUSION

THE testimony examined makes it certain that Augustine immersed King Ethelbert and ten thousand of his subjects on Christmas Day, that Paulinus immersed King Edwin and thousands of his subjects at one time, and that immersion was the mode of baptism commonly used in England till the Reformation. It shows that Clovis, with three thousand soldiers and with many women and children, was immersed by St. Remigius in Rheims, and that immersion was the mode of baptism in France till at least the end of the twelfth century. It shows that the great baptisms of St. Boniface were immersions, and that all succeeding baptisms for about five hundred years in Germany were administered in the same way. It shows that Vladimir the Great and the whole population of Kieff were immersed on the introduction of Christianity into Russia, and that immersion is the mode of baptism universally observed by the whole Russian Church down till this hour. It shows that in Italy, the land of the popes, immersion was the custom of the Roman Catholic Church till the twelfth century had passed, and that the ancient form is still observed in Milan; and it shows that in Spain, Turkey, Greece, Persia, North Africa, Egypt, Abyssinia, and Palestine immersion was once universal, and that in some of these countries it is still the only baptism recognized. *In short, immersion was universal over all the churches of the West for twelve hundred years after Christ, and it is at this hour the baptism of the various sects of the Eastern Church.*

The baptism of the three thousand on the day of Pentecost has often been disputed, because of the difficulty of immersing them; but the missionaries of Russia, Germany, France, England, and Ireland baptized an equal number, or four times as many, at one time, in wells, rivers, baptisteries, or fountains, just as persons were baptized in New-Testament times.

Sometimes immersion is represented as the practice of only an insignificant fraction of Christians. *About one-fourth of all the Christians on earth administer baptism only by immersion now;* and as the whole Christian world immersed for twelve centuries, and a fourth part of it has immersed ever since the end of the twelfth century, *it is probable that a great majority of all the persons that ever bore the Christian name, regarding immersion as the only divinely-appointed mode of baptism, were plunged in the sacramental waters.* So that if truth were established by the number of its adherents, the living and the dead would give us the majority.

The Baptist denomination in this country is increasing at a very rapid rate. With little or no aid from emigration, with an army of prejudices assailing us all around, by the grace of God we have spread over this goodly land, until from 471 churches in 1784 we have now, in 1878, 23,908 churches, with a membership of 2,024,224.[1] We have forty-two colleges and theological seminaries, and fifty academies with instructors of a high order to impart literary and theological knowledge to students of all denominations. We have twenty-nine weekly newspapers, five semi-monthly, and thirteen monthly. We have divinely-honored missions in Burmah, China, Japan, Germany, Sweden, France, Spain, Africa, Italy, and among the white men of the West, and in the Indian territories. We have principles as pure as Jehovah's word, and we have unlimited confidence in their divine Author; and as a result our people plan and foster a spirit of holy

---

[1] For facts and figures in regard to our history, growth, and numbers in this country see *The Baptists in the United States*, by George W. Anderson, D. D., and *The American Baptist Year-Book*, Philadelphia.

enterprise that stops at no difficulty, and that is ready for any undertaking, however gigantic, that promises to honor God; and abounding success has followed our sacrifices and exertions. Our views of the mode and subjects of baptism have entered Pedobaptist communities, and as a consequence the baptism of infants has been declining rapidly for years, and the practice of immersion is believed to be largely on the increase; and the conviction that it is the original mode of baptism, observed by the Saviour and enjoined upon his servants, is now quite common.

Immersionists have no disposition to surrender their revealed mode of baptism. In the East and in Russia the people would make any sacrifice— even give up their lives—rather than surrender New-Testament dipping. In England our honored brethren, notwithstanding the lax views on the Lord's Supper supposed to prevail among many of them, stand firmly where their fathers planted themselves, and demand Bible baptism. In this country our people at this moment are more a unit in utterly refusing any countenance to pouring or sprinkling than probably at any period in our history. One-fourth of Christendom demands immersion for all the servants of Jesus with a resolute voice; and with **the** history of the Church during the *first* twelve hundred years of its existence wholly on their side, with the Scriptures, and Jehovah who gave them, leading on their heroic warriors to battle, their triumph is certain, though for a season it may be deferred. For long ages the doctrine of justification by faith was buried under a vast mass of Romish fables and soul-destroying heresies. This mountain was high and broad and heaven-defying, but the truth under it had volcanic power. In Luther's time the mountain began to heave, the buried power of a Saviour's merits tore an opening from its base to its top, and the laboring volume of burning love, rising up through its hardened strata, burst its sides and scattered them to the four winds of heaven, and sent the doctrines of glowing love over the nations. And now the true mode of baptism is buried deeply from three-fourths of the Christian family. For six hundred long years it has slept in its grave; but, like justification by faith, it will surely spring to life again—the trumpet of the great angel guardian of truth will yet be sounded, and the divinely-given baptism will come forth from the buried past and take its place in all the churches of Jesus everywhere, and one Lord, one faith, and one baptism will become the creed of reunited and purified evangelical Christendom.

INDEX.

A.

ABELARD, 101.
Ablution after baptism, 182, 189.
Abuna, the, 207.
Adgefin, 30.
Africa, North, baptism in, 200.
Albofledis, sister of Clovis, 85, 90.
Alcock, Lord John, Bishop of Ely, 42.
Alcuin, 26, 32, 81, 86, 116, 117, 123, 124.
Alexander, Bishop of Alexandria, 206.
Alnwick Castle, 27.
Alphin, son of Eochaid, 65.
Alvarez, 209.
Amalgaidh, 63, 67.
Ambrose, Bishop of Milan, 56, 102, 119, 137, 141, 201, 202, 204.
America, baptism in, 71.
American Baptist Historical Society, 7.
American Baptist Year-Book, 214.
Anderson, Rev. Dr. Geo. W., 8, 214.
 account of baptistery in Paris by, 91.
Anlaf, baptism of, 37.
Anna, wife of Vladimir, 155.
Annotations of the Westminster Assembly, 47.
Anointing after baptism, 207.
Anointing at baptism, 159, 165, 173, 179, 181, 187.
Anselm, Archbishop of Canterbury, 70.
Anschar, St., 3, 109.
Aquinas, Thomas, 77.
Arator, 144.
Arcadius, 167.
Arians on immersion, 146.
Armenians, 188.
Arnold, Rev. Dr. A. N., 8, 175, 183.
Arrhenius, Claudius, 110.
Arthur, son of Henry VII., 40.

Athalaric, King, 144.
Athanasius, 206.
Athelwold, Duke, 38.
Atticus, 138.
Augustine of Hippo, 3, 18, **19, 24,** 99, 102, 132, 137, 201, 212.
Auxentius, 141.
Avitus of Vienne, 81.

B.

BAPTISM, Abyssinian, 210.
 Ambrose on, 141.
 among the Armenians, 189.
 Arator on, 145.
 Augustine on, 202.
 by H. W. Beecher, 72.
 by immersion, 5, 7, 170, 189.
 by martyrdom, 139.
 by pope at Easter, 154.
 by pouring water, 125.
 Clinic, 134, 135.
 Council of Celichyth on, 34.
 deferred till near death, 110.
 emblem of the effusion of the Holy Ghost, 55.
 Gregory's mode of, 86.
 Hincmar of Rheims on, 94.
 how first administered in England, 32.
 in Athens, 170.
 in the Dnieper, 157.
 in Ireland, 62.
 in rivers or fountains, 124.
 in Russian Church, 159.
 Leidradus on, 93.
 Leo the Great on, 143.
 Lombard, Peter, on, 102.
 Martyr, Justin, on, 140, 193.
 martyrdom a baptism, 139.
 miraculous, 186.
 mode of, 3.
 Munnulus on, 200.
 of Albofledis, 85, 90.
 of ancient Roman Christians, **59.**

INDEX.

Baptism of Athanasius, 266.
  of Clovis, 79, 82, 86, 88.
  of "Constitutions and Canons," 165.
  of converts by each other, 20, 23.
  of Copts, 207.
  of Epidophorus, 204.
  of Eunomians, 169.
  of Greek Church, 6, 52.
  of Hastein, 95.
  of Jesus, 192.
  of Jewess, 130.
  of Jewish proselyte, 190.
  of Mercians, 32.
  of paralytic Jew, 138.
  of pirate, 96.
  of Primitive Church, 54.
  of robbers by Patrick, 69.
  of Saxons, 121.
  of seven kings, 63, 66, 67.
  of son of Prince Milan, 185.
  of ten thousand in one day, 19.
  of twins, 58.
  of upper part of body only, 56.
  place of, 57.
  Pococke, R., on, 207.
  Premasius on, 204.
  profanation of, 38.
  remission of sins by, 134.
  salvation by, 160.
  Stanley, Dr. A. P., on, 151.
  symbol of the grave and resurrection, 94, 98, 107, 131.
  Tertullian on, 196, 199.
Baptist denomination, its increase, 214.
Baptistery in Plymouth Church, 73.
  in Rome, 91.
  of Clovis, 85, 91.
  of St. John Lateran, 152.
Baptisteries, 57, 58.
  at Bradford, England, 59.
  subterranean, 59.
Baptizo, 6, 153.
Basil, 56.
Basilicus, 57.
Bec, monastery of, 38.
Bede, 24, 26, 30.
  on immersion, 33.
Beecher, Rev. Henry Ward, baptism by, 72.
Bingham, Joseph, 54, 203.
Blackburn, Dr., 63.
Blackmore, Rev. R. W., 157.
Blake, Rev. Thomas, 44.
Boniface, 3, 112, 199, 212.
Bradford in Yorkshire, England, baptistery at, 59.

Britons, ancient, conversion of, 18.
Brown, "Hist. of St. Peter's Church of York," 27.
Bruce, James, 209, 210.
Bruno, St., 127.
Bucknell Library, 7.

C.

CAEDWALLA, 32.
Calvin, John, 132, 202.
Camden, 29.
Canterbury, letter from a gentleman in, 21.
Caroticus, or Carodoc, 64.
Cartan, baptism of, 68.
Carthage, Council of, 200.
Carthen opposes St. Patrick, 68.
Cassanus, King of the Tartars, 186.
Cave, William, 134.
  "Primitive Christianity," 49, 57.
Cean Croithi, the Irish idol, 67.
Celibacy, 164.
Chalmers, Dr., on baptism, 48.
Charlemagne, 92, 93, 117, 122.
Child's name not spoken till the moment of baptism, 171.
Christening of Prince Arthur and Princess Margaret, 40.
"Chronicon Alexandrinum," 57.
Chrysostom, 55, 135, 167.
Clark, Rev. Mr., 133.
Clemens Romanus, 57.
Clinic baptism, 134.
Clinics, 126, 136.
Clovis, 3, 79, 80, 82, 212.
Coleman, Rev. Lyman, on immersion, 75, 140, 141, 193.
Coleman of Westminster Assembly, 45.
  called "Rabbi," 46.
Consecration of the fountain before baptism, 123.
Constantine the Great, 137, 152, 164.
"Constitutions and Canons of the Holy Apostles," 163.
Copts, the, 207.
Corbie, monastery of, 109.
Corcothemne, 67.
Cornelius, Bishop of Rome, 135.
Council of Celichyth on baptism, 34.
  of Neo-Cæsarea, 135.
  of Trent, Catechism of, 149.
  of Toledo, 105, 106.
Cranmer, Archbishop, 202.
Croagh Patrick, 67.
Crozer Theological Seminary, 7.

INDEX. 219

Crucifix in the Lady's Well, Northumberland, 29.
Cyprian, 137, 139, 196, 200, 201.
Cyril of Jerusalem, 55, 159.

D.

DELUGE signifying baptism, 127.
Dionysius Exiguus, 56, 166.
Dunstan, St., 35.
Dupin, 22, 82, 103.
Dwight, Rev. H. G. O., 188.

E.

EADBURGA, 199.
Edward IV., 43.
Edwin, King, baptized by Paulinus, 26, 212.
Elfege, Bishop of Winchester, 38.
Elizabeth, Queen, 43.
Elipandus, 93.
England, immersion practised in, 18.
English rear temples in Britain, 18.
Epidophorus, 204.
Epiphanius, 55, 56.
Eric, or Horicus, King, 110.
Ethelbert, 3, 20, 21, 37, 212.
  immersion of, 35.
  wife of, 18.
Eudoxia, 167.
Eulogius, 19.
Eunomians, 56, 169.
Eusebius, 135.

F.

FASTING before baptism, 128, 165.
Felix, 93.
Font, 57.
  St. Martin's Church, Canterbury, 36.
  St. Patrick's, 67.
Fositeland, fountain in, 116.
France, baptism in, 79.
Fridegod on immersion, 35.
Frith, John, 53.
Fulbert, St., 97.
Fuller, Dr. Thomas, "Church History," 20.

G.

GALLUS, Bishop of Clermont, 82.
Garbanus, death and resurrection of, 69.
Gilbert, Bishop of Limerick, 70.
Giles, Dr. J. A., 26, 37.

Gill, Dr. John, 202.
Gocelin, 22.
Godfather in Greek Church, 172.
Greek Church, baptism in, 6, 52, 163.
Green's "History of the English People," 20.
Gregory the Great, 19, 24, 25, 32, 99, 100, 103, 106, 107, 145.
Gregory II., 113, 114.
Gregory VII., 142.
Gregory Nyssa, 166.
Gregory of Tours, 81, 82, 85.
Gualdo, 109.
Gubelmann, Rev. J. S., 8, 130.

H.

HARBOTTLE, village of, 27.
Harduin's *Conciliorum Collectio*, 35
Hastein, baptism of, 95.
Haymo, 100, 124.
Hercus, baptism of, 62.
Hilary, 102.
Hillegenbach, the brook, 111.
Hincmar of Rheims, 81, 88, 94.
Hincmar of Laon, 94.
Holy wells of Ireland, 64.
Holystone, village of, 30.
Horicus, King, 110.
Hugo of St. Victor, 99, 199.

I.

IMMERGO, 211.
Immersion, 165, 213, 215.
  Abelard on, 101, 209.
  Alcuin on, 117.
  Aquinas on, 77.
  Arian theory of, 146.
  Arnold, Dr., on, 183.
  baptisms by, 212.
  Bede on, 33.
  Bingham, Joseph, on, 54.
  Bruno on, 127.
  by Augustine, 24.
  by Beecher, Rev. H. W., 72.
  by Boniface, 117.
  by Clark, Rev. Mr., 133.
  by Copts, 208.
  by heretics, 55.
  by Roman Catholics at Milan, 150.
  by Patrick, 69.
  by the Starovers, 161.
  Calvin on, 132.
  Cave, William, on, 48.
  Chrysostom on, 168.
  Coleman on, 74.

INDEX.

Immersion, Dupin on, 103
  in England in 1644, 44.
  Fourth Council of Toledo on, 106, 125.
  Fridegod on, 35.
  Frith, John, on, 53.
  Fulbert, St., on, 97.
  Gilbert on, 70.
  Gregory the Great on, 119, 125, 145.
  Gregory of Nyssa on, 167.
  Haymo on, 100.
  Hugo of St. Victor on, 99.
  in Abyssinia, 209.
  in St. John Lateran, 153.
  in Greek Church, 184.
  in milk, 70.
  in New Testament, 192.
  in Pomerania, 127.
  in reign of Bloody Mary, 43.
  in rivers, 32.
  in thirteenth century, 78.
  in Westminster Assembly, 44.
  Isidore on, 105.
  Ivo on, 99.
  Lambecius on, 111.
  Lanfranc on, 38.
  Leidradus on, 93.
  Leo the Great on, 142.
  Lombard, Peter, on, 102.
  Luther on, 129, 130, 131.
  Magnus, Archbishop, on, 92.
  Maxentius of Aquila on, 148.
  Maximus of Turin on, 143.
  Maurus, Rabanus, on, 123.
  Milman on, 58.
  of adults in Russian Church, 162.
  of Clovis, 81.
  of infants, 76.
  of Jewish proselyte, 191, 192.
  of three thousand, 213.
  only baptism for those in health, 139.
  only legal baptism in England, 60.
  Philostorgius on, 169.
  Pullus, Cardinal, on, 39.
  Regino on, 126.
  Roman Catholic Church and, 2, 149.
  Rupert on, 128.
  Strabo, Wilafrid, on, 124.
  Theodulphus on, 93.
  trine, 32, 39, 40, 43, 50, 56, 59, 70, 75, 87, 90, 92-94, 97-99, 101, 103, 104, 106, 116, 118, 123-125, 129, 130, 132, 142-144, 147, 148, 159, 160, 166, 168, 173, 187, 189, 195, 198-200, 202, 207.
    not in the Bible, 16.
  only a tradition, 17.
  origin of, 16.
  reasons for, 57.
  Wall on, 51, 53.
  Wesley on, 71.
  when practised, 15.
Immersions recorded by Father O'Farrell, 66.
Innocent III, 142.
Inscription on a subterranean baptistery, 59.
Ireland, 22.
  early baptism in, 62.
Isidore, St., 105.
Ivo, Bishop of Chartres, 98.

J.

James IV. of Scotland, 42.
Jerome, 16, 56, 102, 119, 195, 199, 204.
John, baptism of, 193, 194.
John the apostle on baptism, 193.
Jones, Alfred T., Esq., 8.
Justin Martyr, 140, 193.

K.

Kartzoff, Consul, 185.
Kent, missionaries in, 19.
Kherson, capture of, 155.
Kidnapping of converts, 64.
Kieff, baptism at, 3, 156.
Killala, 63.
Knox, John, 202.
Kohl, 159.

L.

Labbe and Cossart's "Sacrorum Conciliorum," 107.
Lady's Well, Northumbria, 28, 66.
Lambecius, Peter, 110.
Landeheldis, sister of Clovis, 90.
Lanfranc, 38.
Lawrence, St., 125, 126.
Leander, 32, 100, 103, 107, 119, 146.
  letter of Gregory to, 120, 125, 147, 199.
Leidradus on baptism, 93.
Leland, 40, 42.
Leo III., 92.
Leo the Great, 98, 99, 119, 142, 143.
Lightfoot, Dr. John, 45, 190, 194.
Loigles, the fountain, 62.
Lombard, Peter, 102.
Long Parliament, 47.
Lothaire, Emperor, 148.
Louis the Pious, 93.
Luther, 129, 130, 216.

INDEX. 221

M.

MACARIUS, Patriarch of Jerusalem, 159.
McGeoghegan's, Abbé, "History of Ireland," 64.
Magnus, Archbishop, 92.
Maimonides, 191.
Maitland's "Church in the Catacombs," 59.
Maitemquet, the brook, 211.
Malcom, Rev. Dr. H., 8, 150.
Manichees, 201.
Margaret, Princess, baptism of, 42.
Mark on baptism, 193.
Marshall, 46.
Martyrdom considered baptism, 139.
Mary, Bloody, 43.
Matthew on baptism, 193.
Matthew of Westminster, 186.
Maxentius of Aquila, 148.
Maximus, Bishop of Turin, 143.
Meletius, Patriarch of Antioch, 167.
Michelet, 70.
Mikveh, the, 191.
Milan, Prince of Servia, 185.
Milau, sprinkling not practised in, 151.
Milk, immersion in, 70.
Milman on immersion, 58.
Milosh, 185.
Milrita, 204.
Miracle performed by Patrick, 65, 67.
Miraculous filling of a baptistery, 85.
Monica, 201.
Montanists, the, 196.
Mosaic in St. John Lateran, 153.
Mouravieff, 157, 159.
Munnulus, Bishop of Girba, 200.

N.

NEAGH, LOUGH, 68.
Neal, 44.
Neander, 111, 128.
Nennius, 63.
Nestorian baptismal service, 187.
Northumberland, 3.
Novatian's baptism, 135, 138.

O.

OAK consecrated to Jupiter, 112.
Oath taken by German bishop to obey the popes, 113, 116.

O'Farrell, Rev. Michael J., 66.
"Office of Baptism of Greek Church," 175.
Ordo Romanus, 56.
Origen, 163.
Osway, 32.
Othlon, 112.
Otto, Bishop of Bamberg, 127.

P.

PAGANUS, 186.
Parker, Mr., baptism of child of, 71.
Patric, 201.
Patrick, the apostle of Ireland, 3.
  baptism by, 62, 63, 64.
  conversion of, 69.
  destroys the Irish idol, 67.
  fountain of, 65.
  and the robbers, 68.
Paul the apostle on baptism, 54, 55, 132.
Paulinus, 3, 20, 26, 27, 30, 66, 212.
Penda, 32.
Perune the idol, 155, 156.
Peter, 57.
Philip and the eunuch, 194.
Philostorgius, 169.
Photius, 169.
Pius V., 149.
Placilla, Empress, 167.
Pococke, Richard, 207.
Premasius, Bishop of Adrumeta, 204.
Pullus, Cardinal, on immersion, 39.

R.

RABANUS MAURUS, 123, 124.
Regeneration required before baptism, 69.
Regino, 126.
Regnarius, 90.
Remigius, St., 3, 20, 83, 86, 89, 212.
Richerus, 95, 96.
Rimbertus, 109.
Roger of Wendover, 37.
Roderigo de Lima, 209.
Roman Christians, baptism of, 59.
Rowland, Rev. A. J., 8, 152.
Rupert, 128.

S.

SACRAMENTARIUM, Gregory's, 56.
Sadlier, D. and J., 66.
St. Patrick's Cathedral, Dublin, 65.

Salfeld, Christopher, 131.
Samson, an Irish presbyter, 114.
"Sarum Manual," 53.
Saxons, baptism of, 121.
Scandinavians, 3.
Scandinavian immersions, 109.
Sheppy, Isle of, 22.
Sicamber, 85, 89.
Silvester, 85, 89.
Sinn, fountain of, 67.
Sisenand, King, 106.
Socrates, 138, 206.
Sozomen, 206.
Spain, baptism in, 105, 118.
Spring in York Cathedral, 27.
Sprinkling, 132, 149, 151.
    discussed in Westminster Assembly, 45.
    its validity denied by Greek Church, 184.
    sometimes used, 43, 75.
Stanley, Dean, 151, 156, 184, 206.
Starovers, 161.
Statue of Paulinus, 28.
Strabo, Wilafrid, 124, 166.
Swale, the River, in Kent, 21, 22.
Swale, the, in Northumberland, 31.
Sweyn, King of the Danes, 37.
Synod of Vladimir, 159.

T.

TAYLOR, BAYARD, describes a baptism, 170.
Ten thousand baptized in one day, 19.
Tertullian, 15, 56, 196, 199, 201.
Theodoret, 56.
Theodoric, King of Italy, 105.
Theodulphus, 93.
Three thousand baptized by Paulinus, 27.
Tiovulfingacestir, 31.
Tirawly, 67.
Tobur-en-adare, well of, 63, 68.
Todd, Dr., "Life of Patrick," 62.
Trent, baptism in the, 31.
Triforked candle symbol of the Trinity, 171.
Trinity, invocation of the, in baptism, 114, 123, 148.

U.

USHER, Archbishop, 65.

V.

VEDASTUS, ST., 86.
Victor, 204.
Vigilius, Pope, 144.
Vladimir the Great, 3, 155, 212.
    his miraculous restoration of sight, 157.
Vows taken by the candidate for baptism, 58.

W.

WALKER on baptism, 43.
Wall, Rev. William, "History of Infant Baptism," 51.
Wall, Rev. James, 91.
Wash, use of the word in baptism, 113, 114, 115, 140, 145.
Watson, Bishop of Lincoln, 43.
Welsh, Mary, baptism of, 71.
Wesley, baptism of two children recorded by, 71.
Westminster Assembly of Divines, 44.
Whirlpool, 24, 32.
William the Conqueror, 38.
William of Malmesbury, 22, 85.
Willibrord, 112, 116, 117.
Winfrid. See Boniface.
Wooden church built by King Edwin at York, 27.
Woodlock, Monsignor, 66.

Y.

YORK, baptism at, 26.

Z.

ZACHARIAS, or Zachary, Pope, 102, 113, 114.

A BIOGRAPHICAL SKETCH OF WILLIAM CATHCART
(1826-1908)

BY

JOHN FRANKLIN JONES

A Biographical Sketch of William Cathcart (1826-1908)

William Cathcart—"American Baptist pastor, historian, editor, author, cyclopedist"—was born at Londonderry, Ireland, November 8, 1826, the son of James and Elizabeth Cously Cathcart. Reared a Presbyterian, Cathcart became a Baptist at age nineteen in January, 1846, being baptized at Tubbermore (*ESB*) by R. H. Carson, the son of Alexander Carson (Armitage).

He was schooled at University of Glasgow, Scotland and at Horton Baptist Theological School, Yorkshire, England. Cathcart was ordained (1850) pastor of the Baptist church at Barnsley, England and served there for three years (*ESB*).

Repulsed from his native country by anti-church sentiments and attracted to the United States by political ideas, he came to New York November 18, 1853. He became pastor of Third Baptist Church, Groton, Mystic River, Connecticut (December 1853-April 1857). He moved to the Second Baptist Church, Philadelphia and remained there twenty-seven years (*ESB*).

Cathcart was a vocal and committed advocate of Baptist distinctives. He supported the Baptist Union in the dispute over translating the Greek terms related to baptism (*ESB*), advocating that the terms be translated rather than transliterated (*DAB*). He also was a vocal opponent of Sabbatarian views prevalent during his time (*ESB*).

He had conferred upon him the D.D. degree by the University of Lewisburg (1873). He became president of the American Baptist Historical Society in 1876 and continued in that office until 1884. The position facilitated expressing his deep interest in, and devoting his energies to, the study of history (*ESB*).

Cathcart left the pastorate due to failing health (1884) but continued his editing work and historical writing. He prepared a paper on "The Baptists in the Revolution" at the request of the Baptist Ministerial Union of Pennsylvania; the paper became *The Baptists and the American Revolution* (*ESB*).

Best-remembered for editing *The Baptist Encyclopedia* (1881), Cathcart also wrote *Christian Union, Mock and Real*; *The Claims of Large Cities upon the Friends of Jesus*; *The Lord's Day Not the Sabbath of the Jews*; *The Lord's Supper and Unbaptized Participants*; *The Papal System*; *The Progressive Changes of the Infallible Church*; *The Remarkable Preservation of the Hebrew and Greek Scriptures*; *Roots of the Tree of Liberty* (*ESB*); and *The Baptism of the Ages and the Nations* (1878).

He married Eliza Calwell (1850). He died at Guynedd, Pennsylvania July 8, 1908 (*ESB*).

BIBLIOGRAPHY

Armitage, Thomas. *A History of the Baptists; Traced by their Vital Principles and Practices, from the Time of Our Lord and Saviour Jesus Christ to the Year 1886*. With an introduction by J. L. M. Curry. New York: Bryan, Taylor, & Co., 1887.

Dictionary of American Biography. S.v. "Cathcart, William," by William Henry Allison.

A Biographical Sketch of William Cathcart

Encyclopedia of Southern Baptists. S.v. "Cathcart, William," by William A. Carleton.

BY JOHN FRANKLIN JONES
CORDOVA, TENNESSEE
JUNE 2006

THE BAPTIST STANDARD BEARER, INC.

a non-profit, tax-exempt corporation
committed to the Publication & Preservation
of the Baptist Heritage.

CURRENT TITLES AVAILABLE IN
THE BAPTIST *DISTINCTIVES* SERIES

KIFFIN, WILLIAM A Sober Discourse of Right to Church-Communion. Wherein is proved by Scripture, the Example of the Primitive Times, and the Practice of All that have Professed the Christian Religion: That no Unbaptized person may be Regularly admitted to the Lord's Supper. (London: George Larkin, 1681).

KINGHORN, JOSEPH Baptism, A Term of Communion. (Norwich: Bacon, Kinnebrook, and Co., 1816)

KINGHORN, JOSEPH A Defense of "Baptism, A Term of Communion". In Answer To Robert Hall's Reply. (Norwich: Wilkin and Youngman, 1820).

GILL, JOHN Gospel Baptism. A Collection of Sermons, Tracts, etc., on Scriptural Authority, the Nature of the New Testament Church and the Ordinance of Baptism by John Gill. (Paris, AR: The Baptist Standard Bearer, Inc., 2006).

CARSON, ALEXANDER	Ecclesiastical Polity of the New Testament. (Dublin: William Carson, 1856).
BOOTH, ABRAHAM	A Defense of the Baptists. A Declaration and Vindication of Three Historically Distinctive Baptist Principles. Compiled and Set Forth in the Republication of Three Books. Revised edition. (Paris, AR: The Baptist Standard Bearer, Inc., 2006).
BOOTH, ABRAHAM	Paedobaptism Examined on the Principles, Concessions, and Reasonings of the Most Learned Paedobaptists. With Replies to the Arguments and Objections of Dr. Williams and Mr. Peter Edwards. 3 volumes. (London: Ebenezer Palmer, 1829).
CARROLL, B. H.	*Ecclesia* - The Church. With an Appendix. (Louisville: Baptist Book Concern, 1903).
CHRISTIAN, JOHN T.	Immersion, The Act of Christian Baptism. (Louisville: Baptist Book Concern, 1891).
FROST, J. M.	Pedobaptism: Is It From Heaven Or Of Men? (Philadelphia: American Baptist Publication Society, 1875).
FULLER, RICHARD	Baptism, and the Terms of Communion; An Argument. (Charleston, SC: Southern Baptist Publication Society, 1854).
GRAVES, J. R.	Tri-Lemma: or, Death By Three Horns. The Presbyterian General Assembly Not Able To Decide This Question: "Is Baptism In The Romish Church Valid?" 1st Edition.

	(Nashville: Southwestern Publishing House, 1861).
MELL, P.H.	Baptism In Its Mode and Subjects. (Charleston, SC: Southern Baptist Publications Society, 1853).
JETER, JEREMIAH B.	Baptist Principles Reset. Consisting of Articles on Distinctive Baptist Principles by Various Authors. With an Appendix. (Richmond: The Religious Herald Co., 1902).
PENDLETON, J.M.	Distinctive Principles of Baptists. (Philadelphia: American Baptist Publication Society, 1882).
THOMAS, JESSE B.	The Church and the Kingdom. A New Testament Study. (Louisville: Baptist Book Concern, 1914).
WALLER, JOHN L.	Open Communion Shown to be Unscriptural & Deleterious. With an introductory essay by Dr. D. R. Campbell and an Appendix. (Louisville: Baptist Book Concern, 1859).

For a complete list of current authors/titles, visit our internet site at:
www.standardbearer.org
or write us at:

he Baptist Standard Bearer, Inc.

NUMBER ONE IRON OAKS DRIVE • PARIS, ARKANSAS 72855
TEL # 479-963-3831   FAX # 479-963-8083
EMAIL: Baptist@centurytel.net   http://www.standardbearer.org

Thou hast given a standard to them that fear thee; that it may be displayed because of the truth. — Psalm 60:4

www.ingramcontent.com/pod-product-compliance
Lightning Source LLC
Chambersburg PA
CBHW031311150426
43191CB00005B/177